AN INTRODUCTION TO
Z80 MACHINE CODE

ALSO BY THE SAME AUTHORS

AN INTRODUCTION TO
Z80 MACHINE CODE

by

R.A. & J.W. PENFOLD

BERNARD BABANI (publishing) LTD
THE GRAMPIANS
SHEPHERDS BUSH ROAD
LONDON W6 7NF
ENGLAND

PLEASE NOTE

Although every care has been taken with the production of this book to ensure that any projects, designs, modifications and/or programs etc. contained herein, operate in a correct and safe manner and also that any components specified are normally available in Great Britain, the Publishers do not accept responsibility in any way for the failure, including fault in design, of any project, design, modification or program to work correctly or to cause damage to any other equipment that it may be connected to or used in conjunction with, or in respect of any other damage or injury that may be so caused, nor do the Publishers accept responsibility in any way for the failure to obtain specified components.

Notice is also given that if equipment that is still under warranty is modified in any way or used or connected with home-built equipment then that warranty may be void.

All the programs in this book have been written and tested by the authors using models of the relevant micros that were available at the time of writing in Great Britain. Details of the graphics modes may vary with versions of these machines for other countries.

© 1984 BERNARD BABANI (publishing) LTD

First Published — November 1984
Reprinted — June 1986
Reprinted — January 1988

British Library Cataloguing in Publication Data
Penfold, R.A.
    An introduction to Z80 machine code
    (BP.152)
    1. Microcomputers — Programming
    2. Machine codes (Electronic computers)
    I. Title   II. Penfold, J.W.
    001.64'24   QA76.6

ISBN 0 85934 127 5

Printed and bound in Great Britain by Cox & Wyman Ltd, Reading

PREFACE

Home computers are equipped with built-in software that enables them to be easily programmed to do quite complex tasks. The price that is paid for this programming ease is a relatively slow running speed, far lower than the speed at which the computer is really capable of running. Machine code programming entails direct programming of the microprocessor without using a built-in high level computer language such as BASIC. This gives a vast increase in running speed, but is something that can only really be undertaken by someone who has a reasonable understanding of the microprocessor and some of the other hardware in the computer.

Machine code programming is not as difficult as one might think, and once a few simple concepts have been grasped it is actually quite straightforward (although admittedly never as quick and easy as using a high level language). This book takes the reader through the basics of microprocessors and machine code programming, and no previous knowledge of these is assumed. The microprocessor dealt with here is the Z80 which is not one of the most simple types, but is generally acknowledged as one of the most powerful 8 bit devices, and is by no means excessively difficult for beginners. The Z80, or in most cases now the faster version the Z80A, are used in many home computers, including several of the most popular machines such as the Sinclair ZX81 and ZX Spectrum, the Memotech MTX500 and MTX512 machines, and the Amstrad CPC 464. A few simple demonstration programs that can be run on these computers are included in this book.

R.A. & J.W. Penfold

CONTENTS

Chapter 1

THE MICROPROCESSOR

All home-computers are equipped to operate using a high level computer language such as BASIC or FORTH, and these languages are designed to make program design as quick and easy as possible. With most high level languages the programmer uses words that are virtually plain English, and the computer's built-in software then converts these into machine code routines that the microprocessor at the heart of the computer can interpret and act upon. Writing programs direct in machine code is, on the face of it, rather pointless, as it is somewhat harder and a considerably slower process than using BASIC or another high level language to achieve the same ends.

The advantage of machine code programs is the speed with which they run. The speed of a machine code program is, in fact, only limited by the operating speed of the computer's microprocessor, and a computer can perform no faster than when it is running a machine code program. High level languages such as BASIC are inevitably much slower due to the way in which each instruction has to first be interpreted (converted into machine code) before it can be executed. In other words, the program is stored in memory in its BASIC form, and it is only when the program is run that each instruction is converted into machine code and executed. The program is effectively brought to halt during the interpreting process, which accounts for more time than the running of the interpreted machine code. The difference in speed is probably much greater than most people realise, and machine code is typically something approaching one thousand times faster than an equivalent BASIC program.

Action games written in BASIC are often a little sluggish due to this lack of operating speed, especially when a lot starts to happen at once, but a machine code equivalent normally appears to operate instantly no matter how much simultaneous action takes place. With some scientific and business progams BASIC is too slow to be of any use at all, and the use of machine code is mandatory. However, the speed of machine code is its only advantage, and apart (perhaps) from the fun of it, there is no point in using machine code where a program written in a high level language would be fast enough.

There are alternatives to machine code and high level interpreted languages such as BASIC, and we will consider these briefly before moving on to a description of the microprocessor itself. Some high level languages are compiled rather than interpreted. The difference is that with a compiled language the interpreting process is carried out before the program is run. The program may then run using the compiled machine code, or using a sort of pseudo machine code which requires a minimal amount of interpreting. In either case programs should run at high speed, and should be far easier to write than equivalent machine code programs. A compiled language may seem like the ideal solution (and many people would argue that it is), but languages of this type are generally much more difficult to use than interpreted languages when writing and debugging programs, and languages such as BASIC are probably much better for beginners to programming. A mixture of BASIC and machine code (with the latter only being used where high operating speed is essential) can therefore be a more practical solution in many cases.

Incidentally, you may come across the terms source code and object code occassionally. The former is the program in its high level language form, and the latter is the machine code or pseudo machine code produced after interpretation or compilation.

Assembly Language

The terms machine code and assembly language seem to cause a certain amount of confusion, and there seems to be a general belief that they are different terms for the same thing. In fact they are very similar, but there is an important difference. When machine code programming an 8 bit microprocessor the instructions for the microprocessor are in the form of numbers from 0 to 255 (or in some cases, two numbers of this type). This is not a very convenient way of doing things, and it inevitably involves almost constantly looking up instructions to find their code numbers. Assembly language uses a program in the computer to take three or four letter codes and convert these into the corresponding machine code instruction numbers. Most assemblers also provide the programmer with some further assistance, but not much when compared to a high level language such as BASIC. The main function of the assembler is simply to take the three or four letter mnemonics and convert them to the appropriate numbers. An assembler is really the most basic of compilers, but as far as the programmer is concerned there is no real difference between assembly language and machine code, and if you can program in one you can also program using the other.

Of course, the main advantage of using an assembler is that the mnemonics are chosen to closely relate to the instructions that they represent. For example, the Return From Subroutine instruction has RET as its mnemonic which is obviously much easier to remember than the machine code number of 169. If you intend to do a lot of machine code programming an assembler could reasonably be considered essential, since using anything other than a few short machine code routines is generally rather awkward and inconvenient with most home-computers which are designed primarily for BASIC programming. A few computers (the Memotech MTX500 and MTX512 for instance) have built-in assemblers, but assembler programs are readily available for most other Z80A based computers. The facilities offered vary somewhat from one assembler to another, but most give at least some aid with debugging, although they are nothing like as sophisticated as the best BASIC languages in this respect.

One final point to bear in mind is that a high level language like BASIC varies only slightly from one computer to another; and once you have mastered BASIC it is usually not too difficult to write programs for any computer equipped with this language. Problems can arise with the sound and graphics facilities which vary from one machine to another, giving inevitable variations in the sound and graphics commands. However, the language is fundamentally the same for all the computers that use it. Machine code programming is identical for any computers that use the Z80A microprocessor as the central processor. Although there are again differences in the sound and graphics facilities available on various machines, these do not affect the instructions that are available to the programmer (although to produce the desired effect it might be necessary to use a different routine for each machine because of differences in the supporting hardware for the microprocessor). The situation is very different when dealing with a computer that uses a different microprocessor such as the 6502. Apart from the differences in the sound and graphics facilities, the microprocessor will have different machine code numbers for each instruction, and possibly even different mnemonics. For instance, the Z80A Return Subroutine instruction, as mentioned earlier, has RET as its mnemonic, and 169 is the instruction number. The equivalents for the 6502 microprocessor are RTS and 60. Furthermore, the instruction sets of various microprocessors are substantially different, as are the registers they contain and the way in which they handle certain tasks. Obviously all microprocessors work on the same basic principle, but rewriting a machine code program to run on a different microprocessor is not usually just a matter of coverting the mnemonics or code numbers, and changing from programming one type to programming an alternative device usually involves a fairly substantial amount of work.

The Processor

Although a microprocessor is an extremely complex device, usually containing the equivalent of tens of thousands of components, as far as the programmer is concerned it can be regarded as a fairly simple set of electrical circuits known as registers which will perform certain functions if fed with the appropriae instruction numbers. The registers consist of one or more circuits known as flip/flops, and these can produce an output voltage that is either virtually zero, or one that is typically about 5 volts. From the software point of view the voltages are not important, and we can think in terms of low or logic 0 if the output of a flip/flop is near zero volts, and high or logic 1 if it is at about 5 volts. A circuit with an output that can represent just 0 or 1 may not seem to be very useful, and in isolation such a circuit is not of tremendous value, but as we shall see later, a number of flip/flops together can represent large numbers, and can be used to perform complex calculations etc.

The registers of the Z80A are shown in diagramatic form in Figure 1, and the ones of main interest to the programmer are the accumulator (A register), the flag (F register), the six general purpose registers (the B, C, D, E, H, and L registers), and the IX plus IY index registers. The A, F, B, C, D, E, H, and L registers are in fact all duplicated in the alternative register set, but only one set at a time can be used (with instructions being included to enable the programmer to switch from one set to the other as desired). These are 8 bit registers apart from the IY and IY index registers which are 16 bit types. However, as

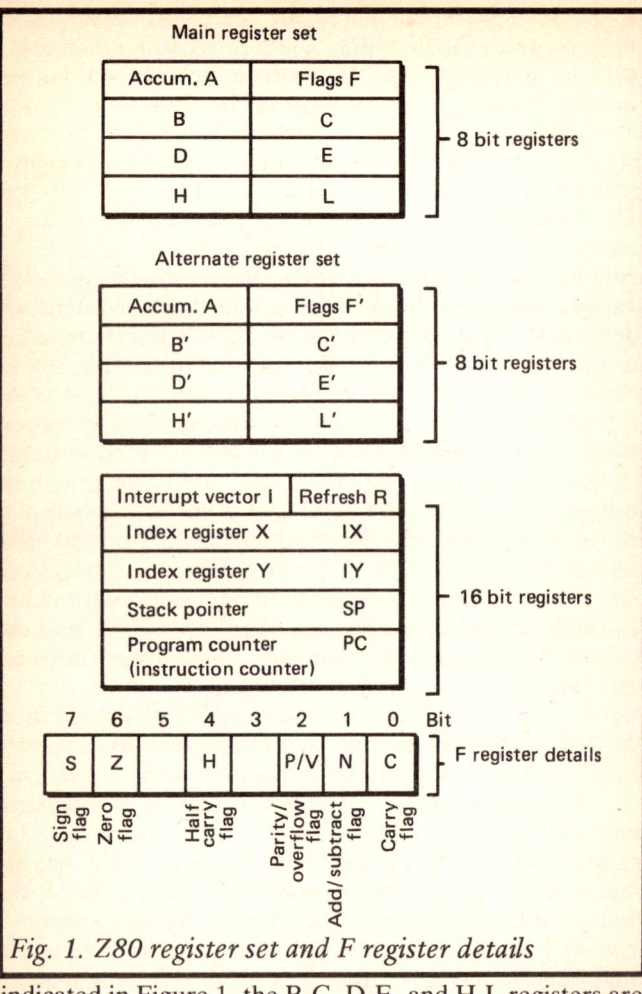

Fig. 1. Z80 register set and F register details

indicated in Figure 1, the B-C, D-E, and H-L registers are paired together, and can operate effectively as 16 bit registers. In other words, they have two sets of eight flip/flops and can handle numbers up to 16 bits long. The accumulator and flag registers also operate together, but, as we shall see later, not in the same way as the other register pairs. Incidentally, a group of 8 bits is usually called a byte, although strictly speaking a byte does not have to be 8 bits long, and can be any length. The point about a byte is that it is not just a collection of unrelated signals or bits, but the bits operate together to represent a number, alphanumeric character, or whatever.

The accumulator is very much at the centre of things, and any data processed by the microprocessor has to be handled by this register and the complex circuit associated with it. With the Z80A some of the other registers can actually be used when processing data, but they are then acting as a sort of pseudo accumulator. The circuit associated with the accumulator is called the arithmetic logic unit, or ALU, but this is something that can be ignored by the programmer. If you feed an instruction to the microprocessor the ALU will almost certainly be involved in the execution of that instruction, but this is something that is all handled internally by the microprocessor itself, and the programmer does not get directly involved with the ALU. At this stage we will not consider in detail the type of data processing that the accumulator can provide, but it includes such things as addition and subtraction.

The IX and IY registers are index registers. Their purpose is to act as pointers to tell the microprocessor where to find data or instructions. In order to understand their function, or the function of practically any part of the microprocessor for that matter, it is necessary to understand, amongst other things, the basic make-up of a computer. Figure 2 shows in block diagram form the general arrangement used in a Z80A based computer. The memory is a bank of 8 bit registers which are used to store both program instructions and data. The number of registers in the memory block varies from one computer to another, but the Z80A can operate with a maximum of 65536. The address bus is 16 bits wide, and these sixteen bits are produced by the program counter (see Figure 1).

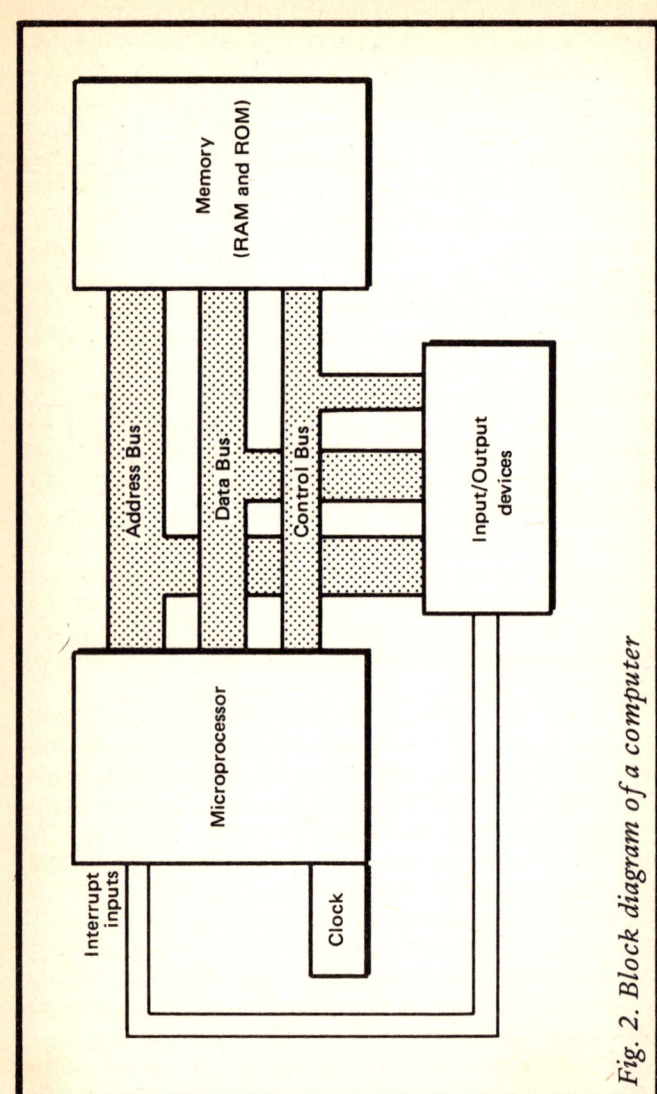

Fig. 2. Block diagram of a computer

8

It is the program counter, via the address bus, that selects the particular memory register that is connected to the microprocessor. The data bus is used to transfer data between the microprocessor and the memory block. An important point to note here is that the data bus is bidirectional, and is used by the microprocessor to take data and instructions from memory, and to place data in memory. There are not separate input and output busses on a microprocessor — the data bus is used for both types of operation.

The control bus is used to make sure that all the elements of the system are operating in unison, and that if (say) the microprocessor sends data to a particular register in memory, that register is ready to receive the data and is not trying to output data to the microprocessor. All the lines in the control bus operate automatically, are not directly controlled by the programmer, and are not something we need concern ourselves with here.

Binary

The 16 bit program counter can place 65536 different output combinations onto the address bus, and it is this that limits the Z80A to 65536 memory registers. Each memory register occupies an address, which is merely a number from 0 to 65535, and each of the 65536 output combinations of the program counter corresponds to one of these addresses. Therefore, by placing each bit of the program counter at the appropriate state, the microprocessor can read the contents of any memory register, or can write data to that register, depending on the type of instruction it is executing. In order to undertake machine code or assembly language programming it is essential to understand the way in which the bits of the address bus (and the data bus) are used to represent a number.

The numbering system we normally use is commonly called the decimal system and is, of course, based on the number 10. There are ten single digit numbers from 0 to 9. This system of numbering is not very convenient for an electronic circuit in that it is difficult to devise a practical system where an output has ten different voltage levels so that any single digit decimal number can be represented. It is much easier to use simple flip/flops which have just two output levels, and can only represent 0 or 1. However, this bars such circuits from operating directly in the decimal numbering system. Instead, the binary system of numbering is utilized.

This system is based on the number 2 rather than 10, and the highest single digit number is 1 rather than 9. If we take a decimal number such as 238, the 8 represents eight units (10 to the power of 0), the 3 represents three tens (10 to the power of 1), and the two represents 2 hundreds (10 to the power of 2 or 10 squared). Things are similar with a binary number such as 1101. Working from right to left again, the 1 represents the number of units (2 to the power of 0), the 0 represents the number of twos (2 to the power of 1), the next 1 represents the number of fours (2 to the power of 2), and the final 1 represents the number of eights (2 to the power of 3). 1101 in binary is therefore equivalent to 13 in decimal (1 + 0 + 4 + 8 = 13).

The table following shows the number represented by each digit of a 16 bit number when it is set high. Of course, a bit always represents zero when it is set low,

Bit	0	1	2	3	4	5	6	7	8
	1	2	4	8	16	32	64	128	256

9	10	11	12	13	14	15
512	1024	2048	4096	8192	16384	32768

Using 16 bits any integer from 0 to 65535 can be represented in binary fashion, or using 8 bits any integer from 0 to 255 can be represented, and this exposes the main weakness of the binary numbering system. Numbers of modest magnitude are many binary digits in length, but despite this drawback the ease with which electronic circuits can handle binary numbers makes this system the only practical one at the present time.

Addition of two binary numbers is a straightforward business which is really more simple than decimal addition. A simple example is shown following:—

First number	11110000
Second number	01010101
Answer	101000101

As with decimal addition, start with the units column and gradually work towards the final column on the left. In this case there is 1 and 0 in the units column, giving a total of 1 in the units column of the answer. In the next column two 0s give 0 in the answer, and the next two columns are equally straightforward. In the fifth one there are two 1s to be added, giving a total of 2. Of course, in binary the figure 2 does not exist, and this should really be thought of as 10 (one 2 and no units), and it is treated in the same way as ten in decimal addition. The 0 is placed in the answer and the 1 is carried forward to the next column of figures. The sixth column again gives a total of 10, and again the 0 is placed in the answer and the 1 is carried forward. In the seventh column this gives a total of 3 in decimal, but in this binary calculation it must be thought of as the binary number 11 (one 2 and one unit). Therefore, 1 is placed in the answer and 1 is carried forward. In the eighth column this gives an answer of 10, and as there are no further columns to be added, both digits are placed in the answer.

Adding two 8 bit binary numbers together produces a slight complication in that, as in this case, the answer is some 9 bits long. When the accumulator is used to add two 8 bit numbers it cannot accommodate the extra bit when there is a final carry-forward, but the 1 in column nine is not simply lost (which would obviously give an incorrect answer and would be unacceptable) Instead, the carry forward is taken to one bit of the microprocessor's status register. Not surprisingly, this is called the carry or C bit. The main use of the status register bits or flags is in conditional instructions (i.e. if the carry bit is set high do this, if it is not do that). Anyone who has done some BASIC programming should be familiar with conditional instructions in the form of BASIC IF...THEN or IF...THEN...ELSE and similar instructions. Note that there are eight flags in the status register, but only five of these are actually used.

Of course, the fact that the accumulator can only handle 8 bit numbers giving a maximum equivalent to 255 in decimal, is not to say that 8 bit computers and microprocessors can not deal in numbers of a higher magnitude. Very large numbers can be accommodated by using two or more bytes together. The usual way of doing this is to have (say) two bytes used together with one byte providing the lower 8 bits of the number, and the other providing the upper 8 bits. These are generally called the low byte and high byte respectively. Two other terms that are often used are least significant bit or LSB, and most significant bit or MSB. These simply refer to the lowest and highest bits respectively (e.g. bits 0 and 7 of 8 bit number).

When adding together two 16 bit numbers the basic way in which it is done is to first add the two low bytes, to give the low byte of the answer. Then the two high bytes are added together with the carry (if any) to give the high byte of the answer, plus a possible 17th bit in the carry flag.

When machine code programming using a home-computer the hardware between the programmer and the microprocessor can help to make things very much easier, but it can also be a hinderance. Few home-computers allow numbers to be entered in binary form, or normally display data in this form, although a few computers do allow data to be entered in binary form (such as the

Sinclair ZX Spectrum using the BASIC BIN instruction). Thus, although the microprocessor would handle a calculation such as 10 plus 20 in binary form, using a home-computer and numbers would be entered in decimal, and the answer would be displayed in decimal. For simple data processing this is very convenient, but when it comes to multibyte numbers and certain other types of data processing it is rather inconvenient. A large number such as 2050 is processed by the microprocessor as two 8 bit numbers, which are entered into the computer as two decimal numbers in the range 0 to 255. In the case of the number 2050, in decimal the high byte is 4, and the low byte is 2, which bears little resemblence to the decimal number 2050 or its binary equivalent. The point to remember here is that bits 0 to 7 of the high byte represent the 512s, 1024s, 2048s, etc., through to the 32768s. However, as far as the number entered into the computer is concerned, when set high bits 0 to 7 only represent 1, 2, 4, etc.

When using machine code you must be aware of the way in which the microprocessor deals with data on a bit by bit basis if you are to fully master the situation, and a reasonable understanding of binary is essential.

Signed Binary

The binary system described so far, which is often called direct binary, is inadequae in many practical applications in that it is unable to handle negative numbers. One way around the problem is to use signed binary numbers where the first bit is used to denote whether the number is positive or negative. The convention has the first bit as a 0 for positive numbers and as a 1 for negative numbers. With this system the normal number range of 0 to 255 is replaced with a range of −127 (11111111) to +127 (01111111). The problem is solved only at the expense of reduced maximum magnitude for a given number of bits.

Note though, that where two or more bytes are used to form a multibyte number, only the most significant bit of the high byte needs to be used to indicate whether the number is positive or negative, and it is not necessary to use the most significant bit of each byte in the number to do this.

Obviously a certain amount of care needs to be excercised when dealing with binary numbers and you must know whether a number is in signed or unsigned binary. For example, 10000001 could be 129 (unsigned) or −1 (signed). In this basic form the signed binary system has practical limitations in that it can represent binary numbers without any difficulty, but calculations fail to give the right result, which makes the system of little practical value unless it is modified to correct this anomaly. It is not used with the Z80A microprocessor in the basic form described above.

To illustraste the problem, consider the calculation:-

16	00010000
−5	10000101
Answer (−21)	10010101

Adding 16 and −5 should obviously give an answer of 11 not −21.

An alternative and related method of handling negative numbers is the ones complement system. Here a negative number is the complement of the positive equivalent. For instance, +16 in binary is 00010000, and −16 is therefore 11101111. In other words, the ones are simply changed to zeros and the zeros are changed to ones. This gives better results when used in calculations, as demonstrated by the foillowing example.

| 16 | 00010000 |
| −5 | 11111010 |

Answer (266)   100001010

This answer may seem to be less use than the one obtained using ordinary signed binary, and the margin of error is certainly greater, but this depends on how the answer is interpreted. The first point to note is that the positive number starts with a zero and the negative number starts with a 1. Provided that sufficient digits are used this will always be the case, and in this respect the system is not much different to ordinary signed binary. The answer is completely wrong of course, but if the carry is ignored the answer is much closer to the right result. It then becomes 10 rather than 11. So what happens if we try another example and again ignore the carry in the answer?

32	00100000
−4	11111011
Answer (27)	100011011

As before, the answer is wrong, but is one less than the right answer (which is of course 28 in this case).

Twos Complement

Clearly this system can be made to operate properly, and it is just a matter of finding some way of correcting the answer. The method used with simple microprocessors such as the Z80 is the twos complement system. This differs from the ones complement system in that once the complement of a number has been produced one is added to it. Therefore, rather than −5 being represented as 11111010, it becomes 11111011. If we now apply this to one of the examples given earlier we obtain the following result.

16	00010000
−5	11111011
Answer (11)	100001011

This time, provided we ignore the carry in the carry flag, we have the correct answer of 11. This is a convenient way of handling subtraction (for the microprocessor anyway) since subtraction can be handled by the same circuit that handles addition. To handle a sum such as 45 − 25 the figure of 25 is converted into (twos complement) −25, and then added to 45. In other words, rather than calculating the sum in the form 45 − 25 the microprocessor calculates it as 45 + (−25), and either way the answer is 20.

The table following shows some sample numbers in twos complement form, and should help to clarify the system for you. Note that, like ordinary signed binary, the first digit is used to indicate whether the number is positive or negative.

Number	Positive	Negative
0	00000000	00000000
1	00000001	11111111
2	00000010	11111110
3	00000011	11111101
4	00000100	11111100
32	00100000	11100000
126	01111110	10000010
127	01111111	10000001
128	010000000	10000000

Note that with 8 bit twos complement numbers the range is from +127 to −128.

So far we have only considered calculations where the answer is a positive quantity, but the twos complement system works properly if the answer is negative. The following example demonstrates this point:-

16	00010000
−31	
	11100001
Answer (−15)	11110001

The system also functions correctly when two negative numbers are added together, as demonstrated by this example:-

−4	11111100
−8	11111000
Answer (−12)	11110100

Overflow Flag

When using the twos complement system there is a slight problem in that a number can be accidentally turned into a negative quantity. The simple calculation shown below demonstrates this point:-

64	01000000
127	01111111
Answer (−65)	10111111

If taken as an ordinary 8 bit direct binary number this does give the right answer, but in the twos complement system the carry forward from bit 6 to bit 7 has changed the sign and magnitude of the number so that an answer of −65 instead of 191 is obtained.

This is termed an overflow, and it is handled by microprocessors such as the Z80 by a flag called (appropriately) the overflow flag. In the diagram of Figure 1 this is given its abbreviated name, the V flag. This flag is actually a dual purpose type, and also acts as the parity flag. This will be described in more detail later. Like the carry flag, there are special instructions connected with the overflow flag, and these can be used to prevent erroneous results from being produced, or to give warning that an error has occured. These flags are normally at 0 and are set by an overflow or a carry forward. They are automatically controlled by some of the microprocessor's instructions, and this helps to streamline things so that he system operates rapidly and uses as little memory as possible. Most microprocessors have instructions specifically for setting or resetting certain flags, but the Z80A has very few instructions of this type, and is designed to operate in a way that renders them unnecessary.

At this stage it is probably best not to go into any more detail about binary calculations and the way they are handled by microprocessors. It is a complicated subject, and it is probably clarified most easily by trying out a few programs which demonstrate the techniques involved. Some simple practical examples that can be run on some popular Z80A based home-computers are given later in this book. Even if you can only understand direct binary, provided you also understand the main principles of microprocessors you should be able to run and understand some simple machine code routines.

Binary Coded Decimal

The Z80A can use another form of binary known as binary coded decimal, or BCD. This is perhaps less frequently used than the twos complement binary system described above, and it has the disadvantages of being relatively slow and uneconomic on memory. However, it can be used to give a high degree of precision, and it can be advantagous in certain applications. It is certainly worthwhile considering this system briefly here.

With BCD four binary bits (often termed a nibble) are used to represent each decimal digit. The system operates in the following manner:—

Decimal Number	Bit Code
0	0000
1	0001
2	0010
3	0011
4	0100
5	0101
6	0110
7	0111
8	1000
9	1001

The binary number is in fact just the normal binary representation of the number concerned, and it is only for numbers of more than 9 that the system is different. The binary codes from 1010 to 1111 are unused, and all two digit decimal numbers require 8 bit binary codes. For instance, the decimal number 64 would be represented by the 8 bit BCD code 01100100. The first four bits (0110) represent the 6, and the second four bits (0100) represent the four. Each byte can therefore represent any two bit number from 0 to 99, which compares to a range of 0 to 255 for a straightforward 8 bit binary number. This helps to contribute to the relative inefficiency of the BCD system. Of course, when a nibble is incremented by 1 from 1001 (9 in decimal) it does not go to 1010 (which is an illegal code in BCD), but cycles back to 0000. A carry forward of 1 should then be taken to the next BCD nibble.

With this system there is no difficulty in handling large numbers, and it is just a matter of using several bytes to accomodate the required number of digits. Negative numbers and decimal points can also be handled with ease by this system, but this requires an additional byte or bytes. This information is usually carried in the high byte or bytes.

Hexadecimal

While on the subject of numbering systems it would perhaps be worthwhile dealing with another system which you will inevitably come across quite frequently, and this is the hexadecimal system. There is in fact yet another system known as octal which, as its name suggests, is based on the number 8. Octal seems to have fallen from favour in recent years, and as it is something you are not likely to encounter these days we will not consider this system here.

A problem with binary numbers is that they tend to have many digits with each digit being either 0 or 1, which makes them rather difficult to deal with in many circumstances. For instance, trying to remember more than just a very few Z80A instruction codes in their 8 bit binary form would probably be beyond most peoples' ability. On the other hand, binary numbers give a graphic representation of the state of each bit in the registers of the microprocessor, and this is something that is often important. Decimal numbers are easier to use in that they are much shorter and are in a familiar form. Converting a decimal number into an equivalent binary one is not a very quick or easy process, especially where large numbers are concerned, and this is inconvenient when it is necessary to visualise things on a bit by bit basis.

The hexadecimal system gives the best of both worlds in that it requires just a few digits to represent fairly large numbers, and is in fact slightly better than the decimal system in this respect. On the other hand, it is easy to convert hexadecimal to binary, and it is easy to use when operating at bit level. The hexadecimal system is based on the number 16, and there are sixteen single digit numbers. Obviously the numbers we normally use in the decimal system are inadequate for hexadecimal as there are six too few of them, but this problem is overcome by augmenting them with the first six letters of the alphabet. It is from this that the system derives its name. The table given below helps to explain the way in which the hexadecimal system operates.

Decimal	Hexadecimal	Binary
0	0	0000
1	1	0001
2	2	0010
3	3	0011
4	4	0100
5	5	0101
6	6	0110
7	7	0111
8	8	1000
9	9	1001
10	A	1010
11	B	1011
12	C	1100
13	D	1101

Continued

Decimal	Hexadecimal	Binary
14	E	1110
15	F	1111
16	10	00010000
17	11	00010001
163	A3	10100011

What makes hexadecimal so convenient is the way in which multidigit numbers can be so easily converted into binary form. The reason for this is that each hexadecimal digit represents four binary bits. Take the hexadecimal number A3 in the above table for instance. The digit A represents 1010 in binary, and the digit three converts to 0011. A3 therefore represents 10100011 in binary. You may find that you can memorise the four bit binary number represented by each of the sixteen hexadecimal digits, but a little mental arithmetic is all that is needed to make the conversion if you can not.

The digits in a hexadecimal number represent, working from right to left, the number of units, 16s, 256s, 4096s, 65536s, and 1048576s. You are unlikely to use hexadecimal numbers of more than six digits in length.

System Operation

If we now return to the block diagrams of Figures 1 and 2, you should begin to get the idea of how data is moved around the system and processed. At switch-on the microprocessor has several of the registers set to zero, including the program counter. The start-up procedure is not normally of interest to the machine code programmer, since few people design their own systems. It is far more likely that you will be using a home-computer where all this is taken care of by the computer's operating system.

The program you write will normally go into a section of memory occupied by random access memory (RAM). This is memory where the microprocessor can set its contents at any desired 8 bit binary number, and then read back that number at a later time. The contents of RAM can be changed an unlimited number of times, but reading the contents of RAM does not destroy the data there or affect it in any way. However, when the computer is switched off the contents of RAM are lost. Software such as the computer's operating system and BASIC interpretter are usually in read only memory (ROM) which retains its contents after the computer has been switched off (although the BASIC interpreter or other language has to be loaded from tape or disc on a few machines). The contents of ROM are fixed, and writing to ROM does not alter its contents. ROM is not an area of memory that is normally used by the programmer, the exception being when there are useful routines there that can be utilized.

The block marked input/output in Figure 2 includes such things as the keyboard and the chip which produces the television picture. Many microprocessors use memory mapped input/output. In other words, the microprocessor reads data from or writes data to input/output devices just as if they were RAM, and they are addressed in exactly the same way. This has the advantage of making programming more straightforward in that using a common set of instructions for memory and input/output operations gives fewer instructions to contend with. A drawback of this system is that some of the 64k (a k is 1024 bytes incidentally) memory address range is occupied by the input/output devices. The Z80A uses the alternative system of having separate input/output and memory maps, but the 16 bit address bus is in fact used for both memory and input/output devices. The difference is in the control bus signals generated by the microprocessor, which select either a memory device or an input/output device depending on the type of instruction used. This leaves the full 64k address range free for memory, and gives more than adequate address space for input/output circuits.

With the aid of the computer's operating system and either the BASIC interpreter or an assembler, the machine code program is placed in a suitable section of memory, and the program is run by directing the microprocessor to the appropriate address. The machine code program then operates by fetching an instruction from the start address of the program, and then shuffling data around its registers and the memory as it goes through the set of instructions. This may seem a rather vague description of things, but if you can grasp the basic concept of instructions and data being taken from memory, or possibly input/output devices, with the data being processed in some way by the microprocessor before being sent back to a memory location or an output device, then you should not find it difficult to understand a few simple machine code programs and then gradually progress to more complex ones. If you can not see how the system operates overall, individual machine code instructions could, to say the least, be rather difficult to understand, and even simple programs would certainly be impossible to follow.

A simple example of how the system operates should now be quite easy for you to understand. We will assume that the program must take a number from some memory location, then add this to a number taken from a second address, and then finally place the answer at a third address. There is more than one way of going about this, and the differences occur due to the various addressing modes that the Z80A can use. In other words, we can place the numbers at any addresses we like, and by using the appropriate addressing mode (or modes) and instructions the program can be made to obtain the numbers from the correct addresses. Addressing modes is a fairly complex subject which is fully discussed in a later chapter of this book, and it will not be considered in detail here. For the sake of this example we will use the most simple addressing mode, which is immediate addressing. With this system the first instruction would be to load a byte into the accumulator from memory (i.e. the first number), and with immediate addressing the byte of data is at the address which follows the instruction. After receiving an immediate instruction the program counter automatically increments by one and moves the program on to the byte of data that is to be processed. The next instruction would be to add the second number to the number currently in the accumulator, and this would again be a matter of having the instruction followed by the number at the next address. Next, the instruction to store the accumulator at the next address would be used, and then finally the return from subroutine instruction would be given. This last instruction simply ends the program and returns control of the computer to the operating system.

This program only uses seven bytes including the one where the answer is stored. Before the program was run these would be as follows:—

Byte 1	Load immediate instruction code
Byte 2	First number
Byte 3	Add immediate instruction code
Byte 4	Second number
Byte 5	Store accumulator immediate instruction
Byte 6	Any 8 bit number
Byte 7	Return from subroutine instruction

After the program was run things would be little different, and the only change would be that byte 6 would have been changed from a random number to the sum of the first and second numbers. In this simple example we are ignoring any carry forward indicated by the carry flag.

It is only fair to point out that the program could not be run in this form on the Z80A as it does not have the necessary store accumulator immediate instruction. However, it could achieve much the same sort of thing using an alternative form of this instruction, and this gives us an opportunity to briefly consider the use of the IX and IY index registers. With the immediate instructions the program counter automatically increments by one after the microprocessor has finished the instruction. This method of doing things is very fast, straightforward, and requires little memory, but it is in many ways limiting.

The IX and IY registers can be loaded with numbers which can then be used to control the program counter in some way so that the program jumps to the required address. In our simple example this indexed addressing is an unnecessarily complicated way of doing things, and they are principally used when working with a block of memory, but it nevertheless illustrates the use of an index register, and should give you the basic idea of how they are used.

Something that will probably have become apparent is that it takes a large number of machine code instructions to achieve quite simple tasks. When programming in a language such as BASIC each instruction is converted into a number of machine code instructions by the interpreter. This is one of the factors which makes writing machine code programs a relatively slow affair.

The Stack

There are a number of registers in the Z80A (and shown in Figure 1) which we have not yet considered, and we will take a look at the function of these now. The one labelled SP is the stack pointer, and this is a sixteen bit register which is used to hold an address. The stack is a set of registers which can be used for temporary data storage, and with some microprocessors the stack is an internal part of the microprocessor. This is often termed a hardware stack. This is in many ways the most elegant solution to the problem, and it has the advantage of high speed. It has the disadvantage of giving only a relatively small number of registers, and does of course add complexity to the microprocessor.

The Z80A, in common with most of the more simple and general purpose microprocessors, uses the alternative of a software stack. This is just an area of memory which is reserved for use as the stack, and the system must, of course, provide RAM at the relevant range of addresses. The stack pointer (the SP register) points to an address in this block of RAM, and with the Z80A the use of a 16 bit stack pointer enables the stack to be placed at any desired section of memory.

The stack uses the last in — first out or LIFO system. In other words, each time data is placed onto the stack the SP register is incremented by 1, and each time data is taken from the stack the pointer is decremented by 1. This is often looked on as being analagous to a stack of plates, with plates being loaded one on top of the other, building a pile from the bottom upwards, and then removing plates from the top of the pile and working downwards. The address in the stack pointer is the address of the last byte to be placed on the stack (the highest address in use in other words).

Apart from use as a convenient temporary data store, the stack is also used when subroutines and interrupts are implemented. We will not consider these in detail here, but in both cases the microprocessor breaks out of its normal operating routine, and branches off into another routine. With an interrupt the signal which indicates to the microprocessor that it must break out of its normal routine is provided by a hardware device via one of the Z80A's three interrupt inputs. A typical application where interrupts are used is the timer that is a feature of many home-computers. Here a counter circuit generates an interrupt (say) every 10 milliseconds, and a software routine is used to increment by one the number stored at a set of memory locations. With suitable manipulation the number in these RAM locations can be converted into suitable data for a minutes and seconds display, or even for a real-time clock. The number can be set to any desired figure so that the clock can be set at the required time. If the timer is to achieve a reasonable degree of accuracy it is important that the microprocessor carries out the software routine at each request without waiting to complete other tasks first. It is for this type of application that interrupts are ideal.

The problem with the use of interrupts is that the microprocessor has to be able to break back into its main routine again after it has finished the interrupt routine. To facilitate this, things such as the contents of the accumulator, the IX register, and the IY register are stored on the stack when the interrupt is generated, and then retrieved again when the interrupt routine has been completed. Things are much the same when a subroutine is called, and a subroutine could be regarded as a sort of soltware generated interrupt. When writing programs for home-computers it is unlikely that you will need to deal with interrupts, and they are principally used as part of the computer's operating system and in a few specialised add-on hardware applications, although you might possibly need to handle them when dealing with the computers input/output devices. Because the computer is continually generating its own interrupts there will almost certainly be restrictions on user generated interrupts, and they may not be usable at all. This is not to say that you can simply ignore interrupts, as in some cases they might affect the operation of your program by producing small but important delays, but in most applications they will not be of any consequence.

Flags

As we have already seen, the Z80A has status flags apart from the carry and overflow types, and one of these is the zero flag (the Z register of Figure 1). This is used in certain conditional instructions, and comparison instructions. The zero flag is set at 1 when the result of an operation or data transfer is zero, and in other cases it is set at 0. With comparison instructions it is set to 1 when a match is found, and to 0 if no match is achieved.

There are other uses of this flag which is also used in conjunction with bit and certain input/output instructions. This is covered in the section dealing with the Z80A instruction set.

The N register of Figure 1 can be a little confusing to anyone who is familiar with certain microprocessors other than the Z80A, since this is the name often given to the negative flag. In this case it is used by the Z80A during some BCD operations, and it cannot be tested by the programmer using conditional instructions. It is therefore only of academic importance to the programmer.

The S flag is the sign flag and this simply reflects the state of the most significant bit of a byte that is being transferred. Remember that with the twos complement system this bit indicates the sign of a number (0 for positive and 1 for negative).

The H flag is the half carry of auxiliary carry flag. This is used to indicate a carry from bit 3 to bit 4, and is needed during BCD operations.

As mentioned earlier, the overflow flag is also used as the parity flag (the P/V register of Figure 1). Parity is mainly used when dealing with text of some kind, and the various characters (upper and lower case letters, figures, punctuation marks, etc.) are then normally encoded using the ASCII (American Standard Code for Information Exchange) code. In fact most home-computers use slight variations on this code, and one or two use totally different codes (the manual for your computer should give a table of the codes it uses). The principle is the same though, with bit codes being used to represent the various characters. The ASCII code uses only seven bits, since this provides up to 128 different characters which is more than adequate to provide a full range of characters. This leaves the most significant bit unused, and free for use in parity checking.

This is very simple in principle, and there are two types or parity; odd and even. With even parity there is always an even number of 1s in the byte, with the parity bit (which is bit 7 in this case) being set to 1 as and when necessary to ensure that the required even number of 1s are present. Odd parity is basically the same, but the parity bit is used to ensure that there is an odd number of 1s in each byte.

The purpose of parity checking is to search for errors, particularly when data is sent to some peripheral device such as a disc drive, and then recovered later. If the data is corrupted and a bit changes state, an odd number of bits will be changed to an even number, or vice versa. However, parity checking is not perfectly reliable, and if two or more bits of a byte are corrupted it is quite possible that a parity check will fail to indicate the error. Parity checking is not used a great deal in practice.

An unusual feature of the Z80A is the R or Refresh register which can be used in conjunction with dynamic RAM devices to ensure correct operation. With most microprocessors this register is provided by external hardware. This is not a register which you are likely to use and a detailed description of its use goes well beyond the scope of this book.

The I register is the interrupt page register, and this is only used in one of the Z80A's interrupt modes. In this mode the I register is used to provide the high byte of the address where the interrupt routine starts, while the low byte must be provided by the device which generated the interrupt.

When dealing with the microprocessors it is common

to find references to pages of memory. For example, you will often come across references to zero page. Pages of memory are simply blocks of 256 bytes, with zero page at addresses from 0 to 255, page 1 at 256 to 511, page 2 at 512 to 767, and so on. The 64k address range of the Z80A gives 256 pages in all.

Z80A Pinouts

The Z80A is contained in a 40 pin DIL plastic package, and it has the pinout configuration shown in Figure 3. The pinouts of the device are really only of academic importance as far as the programmer is concerned, but a brief description of these will be given here as you might find it helpful in understanding how the overall system operates.

The pins marked A0 to A15 are the 16 bit address bus, and similarly, D0 to D7 are the 8 bit data bus. BUSRQ is taken low to set both the address and data busses at a high impedance state. In other words they will simply assume whatever logic level some external device dictates, and will not act as inputs or outputs. The point of this is to give an external circuit (a second processor perhaps) direct memory access or DMA. The microprocessor completes whatever part of an instruction it is performing before responding to a BUSRQ signal, and it then takes BUSAK low to indicate that it has set the data and address busses in the high impedance state. There are two flip/flops in the Z80A (FF1 and FF2) which are set by signals received at the two interrupt inputs of the device, so that interrupts received while the device is disabled are not just ignored. When BUSRQ is returned to its normal (high) state the microprocessor carries on where it left off. It is really a very simple form of interrupt input.

One of the other interrupt inputs is NMI, the Non Maskable interrupt input, and taking this low generates an interrupt, but the current instruction is completed first, and the microprocessor would simply crash if it was not. As its name implies, this type of interrupt can not be blocked by the programmer, and the Z80A will respond immediately to this type of interrupt. The only exception is if the a signal on the BUSRQ line has disabled the Z80A. The NMI interrupt bit is then automatically set by the processor, and the interrupt is serviced as soon as the Z80A is enabled again. The processor automatically stores the contents of the program counter on the stack, and further interrupts are ignored until the current one has been completed. This is obviously essential, since the microprocessor can only handle interrupts one at a time. The program counter is then loaded with the hexadecimal number 0066, which is where the start of the interrupt routine must be placed, or alternatively data and instructions to direct the microprocessor to the interrupt routine could be placed at this start address.

This type of interrupt offers very high operating speed, but it is in certain ways a very simple and rather limited form of interrupt.

An important point to bear in mind regarding interrupts is that the microprocessor only saves (on the stack) and restores the contents of the program counter. If any other registers, such as the IX or IY index registers, will have their contents altered by the interrupt routine, it is up to the programmer to provide a routine to save these on the stack and then restore them again at the end of the interrupt routine. The programmer is also responsible for resetting the interrupt bit of the device which generated the interrupt once the interrupt has been serviced.

The third interrupt input of the Z80A is the ordinary interrupt (INT) input. This can be masked by the programmer and is the lowest priority interrupt input. There are instructions which give three interrupt modes using INT, and these modes will be briefly described here.

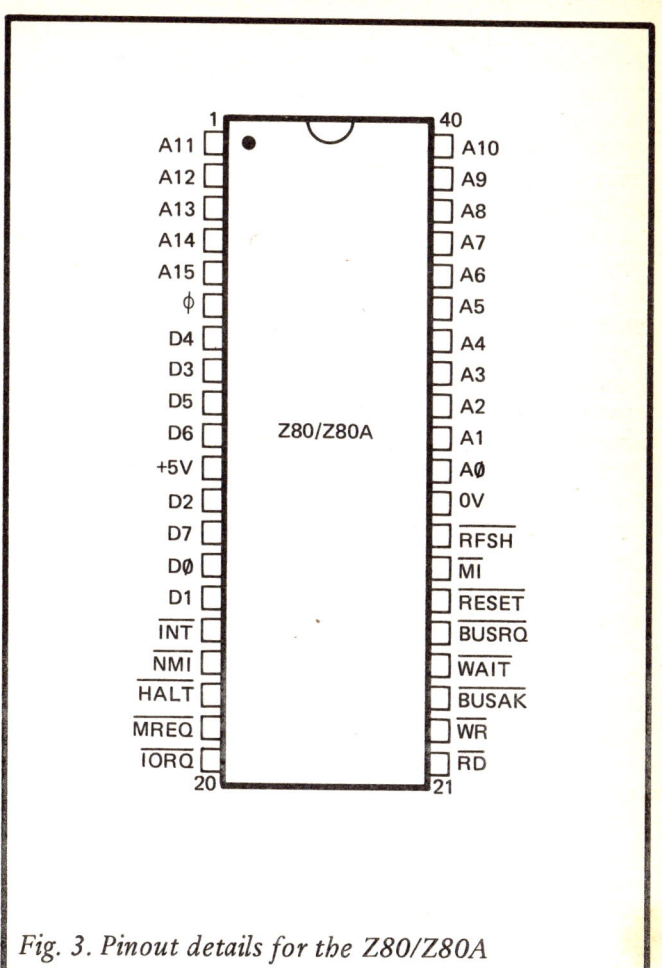

Fig. 3. Pinout details for the Z80/Z80A

Mode 0

This is the normal interrupt mode which is obtained when the device is reset or by using the appropriate (IM0) instruction. It is the interrupt mode used on the 8080 microprocessor incidentally. In principle it is very simple, with the microprocessor waiting for the device which provided the interrupt to provide the next instruction (usually CALL or RST which automatically preserve the program counter on the stack).

Mode 1

This is very similar to using the NMI interrupt, and is a vectored interrupt. In this case the microprocessor automatically sotres the program counter on the stack and then sets the program counter to hexadecimal address 0038. This is where the interrupt routine or directions to the routine should be placed in memory.

Mode 2

This is a powerful but quite complex interrupt mode. The basic scheme of things is to have the Interrupt register loaded with the high byte of an address, and the device which supplied the interrupt supplies the seven most significant bits of the low byte (bit 0 is always 0). This does not provide the start address of the interrupt routine, but instead directs the microprocessor to the correct entry in a table of up to 128 interrupt routine start addresses. This is a fast arrangement with the microprocessor being rapidly directed to the right routine, even though there may be many devices generating interrupts, and many interrupt routines. With most microprocessors, when an interrupt is received an interrupt routine has to be included which checks the interrupt flag in each interrupt generating device until a flag that is set is found, and the source is identified. Interrupt mode 2 of the Z80A is more efficient if a large number of interrupt generating devices are used since it does not waste time polling devices that have not generated the interrupt. It is difficult to implement though unless the special Z80/Z80A peripheral devices are used in the computer.

With this mode the program counter is automatically stored on the stack.

The Reset input is taken low briefly at switch-on, and this starts the microprocesor in its initialisation sequence. It can also be used to take the computer back to this sequence at any time, such as after the computer has crashed. Many Z80A based computers have a Reset or break switch in some form or other, which simply pulls the Reset pin low when the switch is operated. As part of the inialisation process the program counter, together with the I and R registers, is set at zero and interrupts are disabled. The start-up routine therefore commences at address 0000 (but this is the start address of the computer's operating system, and not user supplied machine code routines).

The RD and WR pins are the read and write lines. The RD pin is placed low by the microprocessor when it reads a memory or input output device, and the WR line is placed low when it is writing data to an input/output or memory device. Of course, only one device at a time must output data onto the data bus, and normally only one device at a time must receive data from the microprocessor. Correct decoding of the address bus ensures that only one device is activated at any one time. The MREQ and IORQ lines are placed low to select a memory device or an input/output device respectively. The address on A0 to A15 is valid when MREQ is low, but only A0 to A7 are valid when IORQ is low. In other words, the input/output address range is only from 0 to 255, but some 256 addresses is more than adequate in practice.

The pins marked φ is the clock input. The clock circuit of many microprocessors is built-in, but this is not the case with the Z80A. The purpose of the clock circuit is to simply provide a series of electrical pulses to the microprocessor, and it is these that move the component through the complex sequence of events that make up each instruction. The standard Z80 will operate with clock frequencies of up to 2.5 megahertz (i.e. 2.5 million pulses per second), and it is normally used with a clock frequency at something in the region of 2.5MHz so that it carries out instructions at something approaching the highest rate possible. The more popular Z80A operates at clock frequencies of up to 4MHz, and can therefore perform a given task correspondingly faster. When using the Z80/Z80A (or any microprocessor) in an application where high operating speed is important it must be remembered that each instruction takes several clock cycles, and that a clock frequency of 4 megahertz does not equate with 4 million instructions per second. The number of cycles taken to execute an instruction varies from one instruction to another, but for the Z80/Z80A it is typically about eight clock cycles.

The purpose of the WAIT input is to enable the microprocessor to be slowed down to a rate that can be matched by a slow memory device. The HALT output indicates that a HALT instruction has been performed, and the microprocessor then performs continuous NOP (no operation) instructions until an interrupt is received. MI is an output, which goes low, together with IORQ, when an interrupt has been received. This can be used to acknowledge receipt of an interrupt from an input/output device.

Chapter 2

ADDRESSING MODES

Addressing is the means by which the processor determines, from the instruction, the location of the data, or operand, on which the instruction will operate. The Z80 uses 7 address modes, and in general does not allow combinations of modes. However, where an instruction refers to two operands, it may be possible to use a different address mode for each. Thus an instruction may use absolute addressing for one operand, and indexed addressing for the other.

Many instructions can use more than one addressing mode. Though the mnemonic used is the same for all modes, the way in which the rest of the instruction is written in assembly language is different. The assembler will determine the correct opcode to use from the special symbols or syntax used to indicate some modes (e.g. enclosing items in brackets). When hand-assembling, care must be taken to select the correct opcode, and to provide the correct number of bytes after the opcode. These may vary with a given instruction depending on the address mode in use.

Full use of the available address modes is important to good programming, and it is important to understand them thoroughly.

1. Implied Addressing

This mode of addressing is used only by instructions which operate on one or more of the Z80's internal registers without requiring external data.

All these instructions are a single byte long.

Zilog make a distinction between implied addressing, which is limited to instructions which do not have a specific field to point to an internal register, and register addressing, for instructions which do.

Examples of instructions using implied or register addressing are ADC A,s ; ADD A,r ; AND s ; CP s ; LD r,r′ ; OR s ; SBC A,s ; SUB s ; XOR s.

2. Immediate Addressing

In this mode, the operand is included in the program, immediately after the opcode. As the Z80 has both 8-bit and 16-bit registers, there are two types of immediate addressing, for 8-bit and 16-bit operands. The second, and possibly third, byte of the instruction contains the opcode, followed by the literal, which may be one or two bytes. Thus the total length of some instructions using this mode is 5 bytes.

Examples of instructions using this mode are ADD A,n (two bytes); LD dd,nn (three bytes); LD r,n (two bytes).

When the operand is two bytes long, this mode is referred to as immediate extended.

It is by this mode that constant data is included in a program.

3. Absolute Addressing

In absolute addressing, the location of the operand in memory is specified in the instruction. Two bytes are used, so any position in the available 64k may be specified. This is the means by which variable data may be accessed by the program.

These instructions are three bytes long.

This mode is also called extended addressing, by contrast with short addressing using an 8-bit address.

Examples of instructions using this mode are LD A,(nn), which means load the accumulator with the contents of memory location nn and JP nn, which means jump to memory location nn.

4. Zero Page

In zero-page addressing, an 8-bit address is provided, this being an address in the first page of memory (i.e. the high byte is assumed to be zero). However, this mode is not used in the Z80, with the exception of the RST instruction. This is a single-byte instruction, the effective address being contained in bits 5, 4, and 3. It can thus point to 8 addresses in zero page, eight bytes apart. This instruction is mostly used in interrupt handling.

5. Relative Addressing

With the Z80, this addressing mode is used only with jump relative instructions.

In relative addressing, the byte following the instruction contains a displacement, which is regarded as a signed number between -128 and 127. If the program branches, this displacement is added to the contents of the program counter, causing a jump forwards or backwards. Note that the displacement is the number of memory locations, not the number of instructions.

With most assemblers, you specify the address of the memory location to which the program is to branch, and the assembler calculates the displacement for you.

All instructions using this mode are two bytes long.

Something to bear in mind if timing is critical is that the time taken by a conditional jump relative instruction depends on whether or not the condition is met. If it is met, the instruction will take 12 T-states to execute, as a new address has to be loaded into the program counter. If it is not met, the instruction only takes 7 T-states.

6. Indirect Addressing

In indirect addressing, two bytes following the opcode contain a memory address. The contents of this address, and the byte that follows it, give a further address, which is where the data is to be found.

In fact, very few microprocessors allow indirect addressing, and the Z80 does not allow it in this form. It does, however, allow register indirect addressing, where each of the 16-bit register pairs BC, DE, and HL, may be used as a memory address.

When the registers are used to point to two-byte data, the address in the registers is the address of the low byte, the high byte being at the next higher address in memory.

7. Indexed Addressing

In indexed addressing, the address specified in the instruction is modified by the contents of one of the index registers IX and IY. The contents of the register are added to the address to give the final address from which the data is retrieved.

This is most commonly used to access successive elements of a table.

Instructions using indexed addressing include ADD, CP, INC, RLC and SET.

For historical reasons, all instructions using indexed addressing have opcodes two bytes long.

Chapter 3

THE INSTRUCTION SET

The following list is the full set of Z80/Z80A instructions, including all the variations on each instruction where appropriate. They are listed in alphabetical order, and in addition to the mnemonics the code numbers (in hexadecimal) are also given. Details of any changes to the status flags produced by each instruction are also detailed. Note that a number of Z80/Z80A instructions are two or even three bytes long, plus an additional byte or bytes in some cases (a two byte address following an absolute instruction for example). The number of clock cycles (sometimes called T-states) taken to execute each instruction is included, and provided the clock frequency of the system you are using is known, the execution time for each instruction can be calculated from this. For example, with a clock frequency of 4MHz (4 million cycles per second), an instruction which requires 8 clock cycles obviously lasts 2 millionths of a second (2 microseconds). Do not confuse clock cycles and machine cycles. Instructions are broken down into a sequence of steps by the microprocessor, and each group of steps is called a machine cycle. The most simple of instructions take one machine cycle, but most take more than this. A machine cycle lasts at least three clock cycles incidentally.

ADC A,s

Adds the operand (together with the carry flag) to the accumulator. The result is placed in the accumulator. There are several versions of this instructions:—

Immediate	CE
Implicit (A)	8F
Implicit (B)	88
Implicit (C)	89
Implicit (D)	8A
Implicit (E)	8B
Implicit (H)	8C
Implicit (L)	8D
Indirect (HL)	8E
Indexed (IX)	DD 8E offset
Indexed (IY)	FD 8E offset

The N flag is set to zero, other flags are altered depending on the result of the operation.

Clock cycles, immediate and indirect = 7, implicit = 4, indexed = 19.

ADC HL,ss

Adds the contents of the HL register pair to a second register pair (ss). The carry flag is then added and the result is place in HL.

BC	ED 4A
DE	ED 5A
HL	ED 6A
SP	ED 7A

The N flag is set to zero, H is set if there is a carry from bit 11, the other flags are altered depending on the result of the operation.

15 clock cycles.

ADD A,(HL)

Adds the contents of the accumulator to the indirectly addressed (HL) memory location. Result is placed in accumulator.

Code number   86

The N flag is set to zero, the other flags are altered depending on the result of the operation.
7 clock cycles.

ADD A,(IX+d)

Adds the accumulator to the memory location addressed by IX and offset d. The result is placed in the accumulator.

Code numbers   DD 86 offset

The N flag is set to zero, the other flags are altered depending on the result of the operation.
19 clock cycles.

ADD A,(IY+d)

Adds the accumulator to the contents of the memory location addressed by IY and offset d. The result is placed in the accumulator.

Code numbers   FD 86 offset

The N flag is set to zero, the other flags are altered depending on the result of the operation.
19 clock cycles.

ADD A,n

Adds the contents of the memory location following the

instruction to the accumulator, where the result is stored.

Code number   C6

The N flag is set to zero, the other flags are altered depending on the result of the operation.
7 clock cycles.

ADD A,r

Adds the contents of the specified register (r) to the accumulator, where the result is stored.

A	87
B	80
C	81
D	82
E	83
H	84
L	85

The N flags is set to zero, the other flags are altered depending on the result of the opertion.
4 clock cycles.

ADD HL,ss

Adds the contents of a specified pair of registers to the HL pair. The result is placed in HL.

BC	09
DE	19
HL	29
SP	39

The N flag is set to zero, C flag is reset unless there is a

carry from bit 15, and the H bit is set by a carry from bit 11.
11 clock cycles.

ADD IX,rr

The contents of the specified pair of registers is added to IX, where the result is stored.

BC	DD 09
DE	DD 19
IX	DD 29
SP	DD 39

The N flag is set to zero, C flag is set by a carry from bit 15, and the H bit is set by a carry from bit 11.
15 clock cycles.

ADD IY,rr

The contents of a specified pair of registers are added to the IY register, where the result is stored.

BC	FD 09
DE	FD 19
IY	FD 29
SP	FD 39

The N flag is set to zero, the C flag is set by a carry from bit 15, and the H bit is set by a carry from bit 11.
15 clock cycles.

AND s

The accumulator is logically "ANDed" with the specified data, and the result is placed in the accumulator.

Logical ANDing requires some further explanation. The two bytes are compared on a bit by bit basis, and a 1 is placed in a bit of the answer only if there is a 1 in that bit of both the ANDed numbers.

For example:

Byte 1	11110000
Byte 2	01010101
Answer	01010000

There are several addressing modes available with this instruction.

Immediate	E6
Implicit (A)	A7
Implicit (B)	A0
Implicit (C)	A1
Implicit (D)	A2
Implicit (E)	A3
Implicit (H)	A4
Implicit (L)	A5
Indirect (HL)	A6
Indexed (IX)	DD A6 offset
Indexed (IY)	FD A6 offset

The C and N flags are set to zero, the H flag is set to 1, the S, Z, and P/V bits are altered depending on the result of the operation.

Clock cycles, immediate and indirect = 7, implicit = 4, indexed = 19.

BIT b,(HL)

A memory location is specified using the HL registers,

and then a specified bit of that memory location is tested and the Z flag is set accordingly.

Bit 0	CB 46
Bit 1	CB 4E
Bit 2	CB 56
Bit 3	CB 5E
Bit 4	CB 66
Bit 5	CB 6E
Bit 6	CB 76
Bit 7	CB 7E

The H flag is set to 1, the N flag is set to zero, the S and P/V flags are altered randomly.
12 clock cycles.

BIT b,(IX+d)

This is the (IX) indexed version of the previous instruction.

Code numbers   DD CB offset BIT

Here bit is a two digit hexadecimal number which specifies the bit to be tested, and is the same as the second number in the BIT b,(HL) instruction (see above).

The H flag is set to 1, the N flag is set to zero, the S and P/V flags are altered randomly.
20 clock cycles.

BIT b,(IY+d)

This is the (IY) indexed version or the previous instruction.

Code numbers   FD CB offset BIT

The H flag is set to 1, the N flag is set to zero, the S and P/V flags are altered randomly.

20 clock cycles.

BIT b,r

A register and bit of that register are specified and tested, with the Z flag being set accordingly.

The first code number is CB, the second number can be found using the table following:—

Register	A	B	C	D	E	H	L
Bit 0	47	40	41	42	43	44	45
Bit 1	4F	48	49	4A	4B	4C	4D
Bit 2	57	50	51	52	53	54	55
Bit 3	5F	58	59	5A	5B	5C	5D
Bit 4	67	60	61	62	63	64	65
Bit 5	6F	68	69	6A	6B	6C	6D
Bit 6	77	70	71	72	73	74	75
Bit 7	7F	78	79	7A	7B	7C	7D

The H flag is set to 1, the N flag is set to zero, the S and P/V flags are affected randomly.

8 clock cycles.

CALL cc,pq

This instruction calls a subroutine if a condition is met. Assuming it is, the progam counter is placed on the stack, and the contents of the two memory locations immediately after the instruction code are loaded into the program counter (the first memory location being used as the low byte — the second location being used as the high byte). The program therefore jumps to this address. If the condition is not met, these two memory locations are skipped, and the program continues at the following address.

Condition	Code
Not zero	C4
Zero	CC
No carry	D4
Carry	DC
Parity odd	E4
Parity even	EC
Plus	F4
Minus	FC

Flags not affected.
    17 clock cycles if condition is met, 10 if it is not.

CALL pq

This is the unconditional version of the previous instruction.

    Code Number   CD

Flags are not affected.
    17 clock cycles.

CCF

Complement the carry flag.

    Code Number   3F

The N flag is set to zero, the H bit is randomly affected.
    4 clock cycles.

CPs

The specified data is compared with the accumulator. To be more precise, the data is subtracted from the accumulator but the result is discarded (it is the effect on the status register that is of value).

Immediate	FE
Implicit (A)	BF
Implicit (B)	B8
Implicit (C)	B9
Implicit (D)	BA
Implicit (E)	BB
Implicit (H)	BC
Implicit (L)	BD
Indirect (HL)	BE
Indexed (IX)	DD BE offset
Indexed (IY)	FD BE offset

The N flag is set to 1, the others are set according to the result of the operation.
Clock cycles, implicit = 4, immediate and indirect = 7, indexed = 19.

CPD

This is the compare with decrement instruction. The data in the memory location pointed to by the HL pair of registers is subtracted from the accumulator, but the result is discarded. The HL and BC register pairs are then decremented.

Code number   ED A9

The N flag is set to 1. The Z flag is set if the accumulator and the data to which it is compared match. The P/V flag is normally set, but it is reset if the BC register pair equal zero.

16 clock cycles.

CPDR

This is the (memory) block compare with decrement instruction. The data pointed to by the HL pair of registers is subtracted from the accumulator and the result is discarded. Both the BC and HL register pairs are decremented. Furthermore, if the BC pair equal zero and the compared data matches the accumultor the program counter is decremented by two and the instruction is repeated.

Code number   ED B9

The N flag is set to 1. The Z flag is set if the compared data matches the accumulator, and P/V flag is set to 1 if the BC register pair equal zero after the execution of the instruction.

16/21 clock cycles.

CPI

This is the compare with increment instruction, and the data pointed to by the HL register pair is subtracted from the accumulator, after which the result is discarded. The HL pair of registers is increment, but note that the BC register pair is decremented.

Code number   ED A1

The N flag is set to 1. The Z flag is set if a data match is achieved, and the P/V flag is set to 1 if the BC register pair equal zero after the instruction has been executed.

16 clock cycles.

CPIR

This is the (memory) block compare with increment instruction, and the data pointed to by the HL pair of registers is subtracted from the accumulator, after which the result is discarded. The HL register pair is then incremented, but the BC register pair is decremented. If a data match is obtained and the BC register pair equal zero, the program counter is decremented by two and the instruction is executed again.

Code number   ED B1

The N flag is set to 1. The Z flag is set if a data match is achieved, and the P/V flag is reset if the BC register pair reach zero after the instruction has been executed.
16/21 clock cycles.

CPL

Complement accumulator. In other words, any bits set to 1 are inverted to 0, and any bits set to 0 are inverted to 1 (ones complement). The result is placed in the accumulator.

Code number   2F

The H and N flags are set to 1.
4 clock cycles.

DAA

Decimal adjust accumulator. This instruction is used to conditionally add 6 to a nibble of the accumulator after an arithmetic operation to provide BCD conversion. It will not be considered in detail here.

Code number   27

The flags are altered depending on the result of the operation.

4 clock cycles.

DEC M

Decrements the contents of the specified operand and stores the result back in that location. There are several versions of this instruction:—

Implicit (A)	3D
Implicit (B)	05
Implicit (C)	0D
Implicit (D)	15
Implicit (E)	1D
Implicit (H)	25
Implicit (L)	2D
Indirect (HL)	35
Indexed (IX)	DD 35 offset
Indexed (IY)	FD 35 offset

The N flag is set to 1, the C flag is unaffected, the other flags are set according to the result of the operation.

Clock cycles, implicit = 4, indirect = 11, indexed = 23.

DEC rr

Decrements the contents of register pair rr, storing the result back in that register pair.

BC	0B
DE	1B
HL	2B
SP	3B

No flags are affected.
   Clock cycles = 6.

DEC IX

Decrements the index register IX, storing the result back in IX.

   Code number   DD 2B

No flags are affected.
   Clock cycles = 10.

DEC IY

Decrements the index number IY, storing the result back in IY.

   Code number   FD 2B

No flags are affected.
   Clock cycles = 10.

DI

Resets the interrupt flip-flops, thus disabling all maskable interrupts. (Interrupts are re-enabled by an EI instruction.)

   Code number   F3

No flags are affected.
   Clock cycles = 4.

DJNZ e

Decrements the B register. If the result is non-zero, the

offset value is added to the program counter (signed arithmetic — allowing forward and backward jumps). The offset value is added to PC+2, so the effective offset is +129 to −126 bytes. An assembler should automatically subtract the source code offset value to generate the hex code.

Code number   10 offset

No flags are affected.
Clock cycles = 13 if B not 0, 8 if B = 0.

EI

Sets the interrupt flip-flops, thus allowing maskable interrupts. Takes effect after the execution of the instruction following the EI instruction. Until then, maskable interrupts are disabled.

Code number   FB

No flags are affected.
Clock cycles = 4.

EX AF,AF'

Exchanges the contents of the accumulator and status register with the contents of the alternate accumulator and alternate status register.

Code number   08

All flags are liable to change.
Clock cycles = 4.

EX DE,HL

Exchanges the contents of register pairs DE and HL.

Code number   EB

No flags are affected.
Clock cycles = 4.

EX (SP),HL

Exchanges the contents of the HL register pair with the
top of the stack. The L register is exchanged with the
memory location pointed to by SP, the H register with the
one immediately following.

Code number   E3

No flags are affected.
Clock cycles = 19.

EX (SP),IX

Exchanges the low byte of the IX register with the
contents of the memory location pointed to by the stack
pointer, and the high byte of IX with the contents of the
following location.

Code number   DD E3

No flags are affected.
Clock cycles = 23.

EX (SP),IY

Exchanges the low byte of the IY register with the
contents of the memory location pointed to by the stack
pointer, and the high byte of IY with the contents of the
following location.

Code number   FD E3

No flags are affected.
Clock cycles = 23.

EXX

Exchanges the contents of the general-purpose registers A,B,C,D,E,F,H,L with the contents of the corresponding alternate registers.

Code number   D9

No flags are affected.
Clock cycles = 4.

HALT

Suspends CPU operation. The CPU executes NOPs in order to continue memory refresh cycles until an interrupt or reset is detected.

Code number   76

No flags are affected.
Clock cycles = 4, plus any number of NOPs.

IM 0

Sets interrupt mode 0, in which the interrupting device may place one instruction onto the data bus, the first byte of which must occur during the interrupt acknowledge cycle.

Cycle number   ED 46

No flags are affected.
Clock cycles = 8.

IM 1

Sets interrupt mode 1, in which an RST $0038 instruction is executed when an interrupt occurs.

Code number   ED 56

No flags are affected.
Clock cycles = 8.

IM 2

Sets interrupt mode 2, in which, when an interrupt occurs,
the calling peripheral provides the low byte of an address.
The high byte is provided by the I register. This points to a
second address in memory, which is loaded into the
program counter.

Code number   ED 5E

No flags are affected.
Clock cycles = 8.

IN r,(C)

The register r is loaded with the contents of the peripheral
device addressed by the C register.

r	Code numbers
A	ED 78
B	ED 40
C	ED 48
D	ED 50
E	ED 58
H	ED 60
L	ED 68

The N flag is set to zero. Other flags are altered depending
on the result of the operation.
Clock cycles = 12.

IN A,(N)

The accumulator is loaded from the peripheral device N.

Code number   DB port address

No flags are affected.
Clock cycles = 11.

INC r

Increments the contents of the specified register, storing
the result in that register.

Code numbers:—

A	3C
B	04
C	0C
D	14
E	1C
H	24
L	2C

The N flag is set to zero. Other flags are altered depending
on the result of the operation.
Clock cycles = 4.

INC rr

Increments the contents of the specified register pair,
storing the result back in that register pair.

Code numbers:—

BC	03
DE	13

| HL | 23 |
| SP | 33 |

No flags are affected.
Clock cycles = 6.

INC (HL)

Increments the contents of the memory location addressed by the HL pair, and stores the result back at that loction.

Code number   34

The N flag is set to zero. Other flags are altered depending on the result of the operation.
Clock cycles = 11.

INC (IX+d)

Increments the contents of the memory location addressed by the IX register plus offset d, and stores the result back at that location.

Code number   DD 34 offset

The N flag is set to zero. Other flags are altered depending on the result of the operation.
Clock cycles = 23.

INC (IY+d)

Increments the contents of the memory location addressed by the IY register plus offset d, and stores the result back at that location.

Code numbers   FD 34 offset

The N flag is set to zero. Other flags are altered depending on the result of operation.
Clock cycles = 23.

INC IX

Increments the contents of the IX register, storing the result back in IX.

Code number   DD 23

No flags are affected.
Clock cycles = 10.

INC IY

Increments the contents of the IY register, storing the result back in IY.

Code number   FD 23

No flags are affected.
Clock cycles = 10.

IND

Reads the peripheral device addressed by the C register, and stores the result in the memory location addressed by the HL register pair. The HL and B registers are then both decremented.

Code number   ED AA

The N flag is set to 1. The Z flag is set if B=0 after execution, reset otherwise. Flags S, H, and P/V are randomly altered.
Clock cycles = 16.

INDR

Reads the peripheral device addressed by the C register, storing the result in the memory location addressed by the HL pair. The B register and HL register pair are then decremented. If the B register is not 0, the instruction is re-executed.

    Code number   ED BA

The N and Z flags are set to 1. The S, H, and P/V flags are randomly altered. The C flag is unaffected.
    Clock cycles = 21 for each execution, but 16 cycles only when B = 0.

INI

Reads the peripheral device addressed by the C register, and stores the result in the memory location addressed by the HL register pair. The B register is then decremented and the HL register pair is incremented.

    Code number   ED A2

The Z flag is set if B=0 after execution, reset otherwise. The N flag is set to 1. The S, H, and P/V flags are randomly altered, the C flag is unaffected.
    Clock cycles = 16.

INIR

Reads the peripheral device addressed by the C register, and stores the result in the memory location addressed by the HL register pair. The B register is then decremented and the HL register pair is incremented. If B is not zero, the instruction is re-executed.

    Code number   ED B2

The Z flag is set if B=0 after execution, reset otherwise. The N flag is set to 1. The S, H, and P/V flags are randomly altered, the C flag is unaffected.

Clock cycles = 21 for each execution, but 16 only when B = 0.

JP cc,pq

Tests the condition cc. If true, program execution continues from address pq (low byte — high byte). If the condition is not true, program execution continues with the next instruction in sequence.

cc	Code numbers	
NZ	C2 low byte high byte	NON ZERO
Z	CA low byte high byte	ZERO
NC	D2 low byte high byte	NO CARRY
C	DA low byte high byte	CARRY
PO	E2 low byte high byte	PARITY ODD
PE	EA low byte high byte	PARITY EVEN
P	F2 low byte high byte	P SIGN POSITIVE
M	FA low byte high byte	SIGN NEGATIVE

No flags are affected.
Clock cycles=10.

JP pq

Causes an unconditional jump to memory location pq. The next instruction will be fetched from this address.

Code number   C3 address low byte —
                     address high byte

No flags are affected.
Clock cycles = 10.

JP (HL)

Causes an unconditional jump to the address stored in the HL register pair. The next instruction is fetched from this address.

Code number   E9

No flags are affected.
Clock cycles = 4.

JP (IX)

Causes an unconditional jump to the address stored in IX. The next instruction is fetched from this address.

Code number   DD E9

No flags are affected.
Clock cycles = 8.

JP (IY)

Causes an unconditional jump to the address stored in IY. The next instruction is fetched from this address.

Code number   FD E9

No flags are affected.
Clock cycles = 8.

JR cc,e

Tests the condition cc. If true, the offset e is added to the program counter (signed arithmetic — forward and backward jumps possible). The offset is added to PC+2, so the effective range is +129 to –126 bytes. If the condition is not met, the next instruction in sequence is executed.

cc	Code numbers
NZ	20 offset
Z	28 offset
NC	30 offset
C	38 offset

No flags are affected.
Clock cycles; condition met = 12, condition not met = 7.

JR e

Causes an unconditional jump by the offset e. The offset e is added to the program counter (signed arithmetic) and the next instruction is fetched from this address. The offset is added to PC+2, so the effective range is +129 to −126 bytes.

Code number	18 offset

No flags are affected.
Clock cycles = 12.

LDdd,(nn)

The two bytes which follow the instruction code point to a memory location, the contents of which is loaded into the low order of the specified register pair. The contents of the following memory location is loaded into the high order of the specified register pair. The low byte of the address is the one which immediately follows the instruction code.

BC	ED 4B
DE	ED 5B
HL	ED 6B
SP	ED 7B

The flags are not affected.
20 clock cycles.

LDdd,nn

Loads the contents of the two memory locations immediately following the instruction code into the specified register pair (the low byte is the first one after the instruction code).

BC	01
DE	11
HL	21
SP	31

The flags are not affected.
10 clock cycles.

LDr,n

This is the load register (r) immediate instruction. The specified register is loaded with the contents of the memory location immediately after the one containing the instruction code.

A	3E
B	06
C	0E
D	16
E	1E
H	26
L	2E

The flags are not affected.
7 clock cycles.

LDr,r′

The load register (r) from register (r′) instruction. The contents of one specified register are loaded into a second specified register.

Source Register	A	B	C	D	E	H	L
Destination							
A	7F	78	79	7A	7B	7C	7D
B	47	40	41	42	43	44	45
C	4F	48	49	4A	4B	4C	4D
D	57	50	51	52	53	54	55
E	5F	58	59	5A	5B	5C	5D
H	67	60	61	62	63	64	65
L	6F	68	69	6A	6B	6C	6D

The flags are not affected.
   4 clock cycles.

LD(BC),A

Loads the data in the accumulator into the memory location pointed to by the BC register pair.

   Code number   02

The flags are not affected.
   7 clock cycles.

LD(DE),A

Loads the data in the accumulator into the memory location pointed to by the DE register pair.

   Code number   12

The flags are not affected.
7 clock cycles.

LD(HL),n

Loads the contents of the memory location immediately after the instruction code into the memory location pointed to by the HL register pair.

Code number   36

The flags are not affected.
10 clock cycles.

LD(HL),r

Loads the contents of the specified register into the memory location pointed to by the HL register pair.

A	77
B	70
C	71
D	72
E	73
H	74
L	75

The flags are not affected.

7 clock cycles.

LDr,(IX+d)

Loads the contents of the memory location addressed by the IX register plus the given offset, into the specified register.

A	DD 7E offset
B	DD 46 offset
C	DD 4E offset
D	DD 56 offset
E	DD 5E offset
H	DD 66 offset
L	DD 6E offset

The flags are not affected.
19 clock cycles.

LDr,(IY+d)

Loads the contents of the memory location addressed by the IY register plus the given offset, into the specified register.

A	FD 7E offset
B	FD 46 offset
C	FD 4E offset
D	FD 56 offset
E	FD 5E offset
H	FD 66 offset
L	FD 6E offset

The flags are not affected.
19 clock cycles.

LD(IX+d),n

The immediate data is loaded into the memory location addressed by the IX register plus the given offset. The immediate data follows the offset value.

| Code number | DD 36 offset |

The flags are not affected.
19 clock cycles.

LD(IY+d),n

The immediate data is loaded into the memory location addressed by the IY register plus the given offset. The immediate data follows the offset value.

Code number   FD 36 offset

The flags are not affected.
19 clock cycles.

LD(IX+d),r

Loads the contents of the specified register into the memory location pointed to by the IX register and the given offset.

A	DD 77 offset
B	DD 70 offset
C	DD 71 offset
D	DD 72 offset
E	DD 73 offset
H	DD 74 offset
L	DD 75 offset

The flags are not affected.
19 clock cycles.

LD(IY+d),r

Loads the contents of the specified register into the memory location pointed to by the IY register and the given offset.

A	FD 77 offset
B	FD 70 offset
C	FD 71 offset
D	FD 72 offset
E	FD 73 offset
H	FD 74 offset
L	FD 75 offset

The flags are not affected.
19 clock cycles.

LDA,(nn)

Loads the accumulator from the address provided by the two bytes following the instruction code. The low byte of the address is the first one after the instruction code.

Code number   3A

The flags are not affected.
13 clock cycles.

LD(nn),A

Loads the data in the accumulator into the address given in the two bytes following the instruction code. The low byte of the address is the first one after the instruction code.

Code number   32

The flags are not affected.
13 clock cycles.

LD(nn),dd

Loads the low byte from the specified register pair into the memory location specified by the two bytes following the instruction code. The high byte is loaded into the address following the one specified. The low byte of the address is the one following immediately after the instruction code.

BC	ED 43
DE	ED 53
HL	ED 63
SP	ED 73

The flags are not affected.
20 clock cycles.

LD(nn),HL

Loads the data in the L register into the memory location specified by the two bytes following the instruction code (the first byte being the low order one of the address). The contents of the H register are loaded into the memory location following the specified address.

Code number   22

The flags are not affected.
16 clock cycles.

LD(nn),IX

Loads the data in the low order of the IX register into the memory location specified by the two bytes following the instruction code (the first byte being the low order one of the address). The contents of the high order of the IX register are loaded into the memory location following the specified address.

Code number   DD 22

The flags are not affected.
   20 clock cycles.

LD(nn),IY

Loads the data in the low order of the IY register into the memory location specified by the two bytes following the instruction code (the first byte being the low order one of the address). The contents of the high order of the IY register are loaded into the memory location following the specified address.

Code number   FD 22

The flags are not affected.
   20 clock cycles.

LDA,(BC)

Data in the memory location pointed to by the BC register pair is loaded into the accumulator.

Code number   0A

The flags are not affected.
   7 clock cycles.

LDA,(DE)

Data in the memory location pointed to by the DE register pair is loaded into the accumulator.

Code number   1A

The flags are not affected.
   7 clock cycles.

LDA,I

Loads the contents of the interrupt vector register into the accumulator.

Code number ED 57

The H and N flags are set to 0, the P/V flag is set to the state of the interrupt flag IFF2, and the S and Z flags are altered depending on the result of the operation.
9 clock cycles.

LDI,A

Loads the data in the accumulator into the interrupt vector register.

Code number ED 47

The flags are not affected.
9 clock cycles.

LDA,R

Loads the contents of the R register into the accumulator.

Code number ED 5F

The H and N flags are set to zero, and P/V flag is set to the same state as the IFF2 interrupt flag, and the S and Z flags are altered depending on the result of the operation.
9 clock cycles.

LD HL,(nn)

The two bytes following the instruction code specify a memory location. The contents of this location are loaded into the L register. The contents of the memory location following the specified one are loaded into the H register. The low byte of the specified address is the one immediately after the instruction code.

Code number   2A

The flags are not affected.
   16 clock cycles.

LD IX,nn

Loads the IX register with the two bytes of data immediately following the instruction code (the low order byte is the first one after the instruction code).

Code number   DD 21

The flags are not affected.
   14 clock cycles.

LD IX,(nn)

The two bytes following the instruction code specify the address from which the low order of the IX register is loaded. The high order of the IX register is loaded from the memory location following the specified address. The low byte of the specified address is the one which immediately follows the instruction code.

Code number   DD 2A

The flags are not affected.
   20 clock cycles.

LD IY,nn

The IY register is loaded with the data in the two memory locations following the instruction code (the low order byte being the first one after the instruction code).

Code number   FD 21

The flags are not affected.
14 clock cycles.

LD IY,(nn)

The two bytes following the instruction code specify an address. The contents of this address are loaded into the low order of the IY register. The contents of the address following the specified address are loaded into the high order of the IY register. The low byte of the address is the one immeditely after the instruction code.

Code number   FD 2A

The flags are not affected.
20 clock cycles.

LD R,A,

Loads the contents of the accumulator into the R register.

Code number   ED 4F

The flags are not affected.
9 clock cycles.

LD SP,HL

Loads the data in the HL register pair into the SP register.

Code number   F9

The flags are not affected.
6 clock cycles.

LD SP,IX

Loads the data in IX register into the SP register.

Code number   DD F9

The flags are not affected.
10 clock cycles.

LD SP,IY

Loads the data in the IY register into the SP register.

Code number   FD F9

The flags are not affected.
10 clock cycles.

LDD

This is the (memory) block load with decrement instruction. The contents of the memory location pointed to by the HL register pair are loaded into the memory location addressed by the DE register pair. The BC, DE, and HL register pairs are then all decremented.

Code number   ED A8

The H and N flags are set to zero. The P/V flag is set to zero if BC equals zero after the instruction has been executed.
16 clock cycles.

LDDR

This is the repeating (memory) block load with decrement instruction. It loads the data in the memory location pointed to by the HL register pair into the memory location addressed by the DE register pair. The BC, DE, and HL register pairs are all then decremented. If BC is not equal to zero the program counter is decremented by two and the instruction is repeated.

Code number   ED B8

The H, N, and P/V flags are all set to zero.
16/21 clock cycles.

LDI

This is the (memory) block load with increment instruction. The data in the memory location pointed to by the HL register pair are loaded into the address pointed to by the DE register pair. The DE and HL register pairs are then incremented, but the BC register pair is decremented.

Code number   ED A0

The H and N flags are set to zero. The P/V flag is set to zero if the BC register pair equals zero after the instruction has been executed.
16 clock cycles.

LDIR

This is the repeating (memory) block load with increment instruction. The data in the memory location pointed to by the HL registers is loaded into the memory location pointed to by the DE registers. The DE and HL registers are then incremented, but the BC register is decremented. If BC is not equal to zero the program counter is then decremented by two and the instruction is executed again.

Code number   ED B0

The H, N, and P/V flags are all set to zero.
  16/21 clock cycles.

LDr,(HL)

Loads the contents of the memory location pointed to by the HL registers into the specified register.

A	7E
B	46
C	4E
D	56
E	5E
H	66
L	6E

The flags are not affected.
  7 clock cycles.

NEG

This is the negate the accumulator instruction. It subtracts the contents of the accumulator from zero and places the result in the accumulator (twos complements the accumulator in other words).

  Code number   ED 44

The C bit will be set if the accumulator was zero before the instruction was executed, and the P/V flag will be set if the accumulator was 80 (hexadecimal).
  8 clock cycles.

NOP

This is the no operation instruction, and it simply provides a delay of four clock cycles.

Code number   00

ORs

This instruction logically ORs the specified data with the data in the accumulator, and places the result in the accumulator. Logical ORing compares the two pieces of data on a bit by bit basis, and places a 1 in a bit of the answer if there is a 1 in that bit of the first number or the second one. The example given below demonstrates this.

First number	11110000
Second number	01010101
Answer	11110101
Implicit (A)	B7
Implicit (B)	B0
Implicit (C)	B1
Implicit (D)	B2
Implicit (E)	B3
Implicit (H)	B4
Implicit (L)	B5
Immediate	F6
Indirect (HL)	B6
Indexed (IX)	DD B6 offset
Indexed (IY)	FD B6 offset

The H, N, and C flags are set to zero, the other flags are altered depending on the result of the operation.

Clock cycles, Implicit = 4, immediate and indirect = 7, indexed = 19.

OTDR

This is the block output with decrement instruction. The HL register pair point to a memory location, the contents of which are transferred to the output device addressed by the C register. This is followed by the HL register pair and the B register being decremented. If the B register is not equal to zero the program counter is decremented by two and the instruction is repeated.

Code number   ED BB

The Z and N flags are set to one, and the other flags are randomly affected.
16/21 clock cycles.

OTIR

This is the block output with increment instruction. The HL register pair point to a memory location, the contents of which are transferred to the output device addressed by the contents of the C register. Then the B register is decremented but the HL register pair is incremented. If the B register is not equal to zero the program counter is decremented by two and the instruction is repeated.

Code number   ED B3

The Z and N flags are set to 1, and the other flags are randomly affected.
16/21 clock cycles.

OUT(C),r

This instruction transfer the contents of the specified register to the output device addressed by the contents of the C register.

A	ED 79
B	ED 41
C	ED 49
D	ED 51
E	ED 59
H	ED 61
L	ED 69

The flags are not affected.
12 clock cycles.

OUT(N),A

This instruction transfers the contents of the accumulator to the output device addressed by the memory location immediately following the instruction code.

Code number   D3

The flags are not affected.
11 clock cycles.

OUTD

This instruction transfers the contents of the memory location pointed to by the HL register pair to the output device addressed by the C register. The HL register pair and the B register are then decremented.

Code number   ED AB

The N flag is set to 1, and the S, H, and P/V flags are randomly affected. The Z flag is set if the B register equals zero after execution of the instruction.
16 clock cycles.

OUTI

This instruction transfer the contents of the memory location pointed to by the HL register pair to the output device addressed by the C register. The HL register pair is then incremented, but the B register is decremented.

Code number   ED A3

The N flag is set to 1, and the S, H, and P/V flags are randomly affected. The Z flag is set if the B register equals zero after execution of the instruction.

16 clock cycles.

POPqq

The data in the memory location addressed via the stack pointer is loaded into the low order of the specified register pair. Then the stack pointer is incremented, and the contents of the memory location then addressed via the stack pointer is loaded into the high order of the specified register pair. The stack pointer is then incremented again.

BC	C1
DE	D1
HL	E1
AF	F1

The flags are not affected.

10 clock cycles.

POP IX

The data in the memory location addressed via the stack pointer is loaded into the low order of the IX register. Then the stack pointer is incremented, and the contents of the memory location addressed via this register are loaded into the high order of the IX register. The stack pointer is then incremented again.

Code number   DD E1

The flags are not affected.
    14 clock cycles.

POP IY

The data in the memory location addressed via the stack pointer is loaded into the low order of the IY register. Then the stack pointer is incremented, and the contents of the memory location addressed via this register are loaded into the high order of the IY register. The stack pointer is then incremented again.

    Code number   FD E1

The flags are not affected.
    14 clock cycles.

PUSH qq

First the stack pointer is decremented, and the high order of the specified pair of registers is transferred to the memory location addressed via the stack pointer. After a further decrementation of the stack pointer, the contents of the low order of the specified register pair are loaded into the memory location addressed via the stack pointer.

BC	C5
DE	D5
HL	E5
AF	F5

The flags are not affected.
    11 clock cycles.

PUSH IX

First the stack pointer is decremented, and then the contents of the high order of the IX register are loaded into the memory location addressed via the stack pointer. After the stack pointer has been decremented again, the contents of the low order of the IX register are loaded into the memory location addressed via the stack pointer.

    Code number   DD E5

The flags are not affected.
    15 clock cycles.

PUSH IY

First the stack pointer is decremented, and then the contents of the high order of the IY register are loaded into the memory location addressed via the stack pointer. After the stack pointer has been decremented again, the contents of the low order of the IY register are loaded into the memory location addressed via the stack pointer.

    Code number   FD E5

The flags are not affected.
    15 clock cycles.

RES b,r

This instruction is used to reset the specified bit of a specified register, as detailed in the table provided. Note that this only gives the second byte of the instruction's code number: the first byte is always CB.

	A	B	C	D	E	H	L
0	87	80	81	82	83	84	85
1	8F	88	89	8A	8B	8C	8D
2	97	90	91	92	93	94	95
3	9F	98	99	9A	9B	9C	9D
4	A7	A0	A1	A2	A3	A4	A5
5	AF	A8	A9	AA	AB	AC	AD
6	B7	B0	B1	B2	B3	B4	B5
7	BF	B8	B9	BA	BB	BC	BD

The flags are not affected.
   8 clock cycles.

RES b,(rr)

This instruction is used to reset the specified bit of the specified memory location.

	0	1	2	3	4	5	6	7
Indirect (HL)	86	8E	96	9E	A6	AE	B6	BE

This list gives the second byte: the first byte of the instruction is CB.

Indexed (IX)	The list given above provides the third byte: the first and second bytes of the instruction code are DD and CB.
Indexed (IY)	The list given above provides the third byte; the first and second bytes of the instruction code are FD and CB.

The flags are not affected.
   Clock cycles, Indirect = 15, indexed = 23.

RET

This is the return from subroutine instruction. This "POPs" the program counter from the stack, and then the program continues at the memory location addressed by the program counter.

    Instruction code   C9

The flags are not affected.
    10 clock cycles.

RET cc

Returns from subroutine if condition cc is met. If the condition is met, the program counter is loaded from the stack, and the next instruction fetched from this address. If the condition is not met, the next instruction in sequence is executed.

cc	Code number
NZ	C0
Z	C8
NC	D0
C	D8
PO	E0
PE	E8
P	F0
M	F8

No flags are affected.
    Clock cycles; condition met = 11, condition not met = 5.

RETI

This instruction is recognised by Zilog peripherals as the

end of a peripheral servicing routine. Its use allows proper control of a system of nested priority interrupts. The program counter is loaded from the stack, and the next instruction is fetched from this address. An EI instruction should be used before RETI to re enable interrupts.

Code number   ED 4D

No flags are affected.
   Clock cycles = 14.

RETN

Return from a non-maskable interrupt. The program counter is loaded from the stack, and the state of the interrupt flag is restored to what it was before the non-maskable interrupt.

Code number   ED 45

No flags are affected.
   Clock cycles = 14.

RL s

Rotates the contents of the operand s one bit position to the left. The carry flag is effectively used as the ninth bit, the contents of the carry flag being moved into bit 0, and the contents of bit 7 going into the carry flag. The result is stored back in the original location.
   There are several versions of this instruction.

Implicit A	CB 17
Implicit B	CB 10
Implicit C	CB 11
Implicit D	CB 12

Implicit E	CB 13
Implicit H	CB 14
Implicit L	CB 15
Indirect (HL)	CB 16
Indexed (IX+d)	DD CB offset 16
Indexed (IY+d)	FD CB offset 16

Flags H and N are set to zero, C is set by bit 7 of source, other flags are altered depending on the result of the operation.

Clock cycles; implicit = 8, indirect = 15, indexed = 23.

RLA

Rotates the contents of the accumulator one bit to the left, the result being stored back in the accumulator. The carry flag is used as a ninth bit.

Code number   17

The H and N flags are set to zero. The carry flag is set by bit 7 of accumulator. Other flags are not affected.
Clock cycles = 4.

RLCA

Rotates the contents of the accumulator one bit position to the left. The contents of bit 7 are copied into bit 0 and the carry flag. This instruction is the same as RLC A, except for the effect on flags.

Code number   07

The H and N flags are set to 0. The carry flag is set by bit 7 of accumulator. Other flags are not affected.
Clock cycles = 4.

NB. This instruction is included for compatibility with the 8080 processor.

RLC r

Rotates the contents of register r left one bit position. The contents of bit 7 are copied into bit 0 and the carry flag.

Register code numbers

A	CB 07
B	CB 00
C	CB 01
D	CB 02
E	CB 03
H	CB 04
L	CB 05

The H and N flags are set to zero. The carry flag is set by bit 7 of the register. Other flags are altered according to the result of the operation.
Clock cycles = 8.

RLC (HL)

Rotates the contents of the memory location addressed by the HL register pair one bit position to the left. The result is stored back at that location. The contents of bit 7 are copied into the carry flag and bit 0.

Code number   CB 06

The H and N flags are set to 0. The carry flag is set by bit 7 of the memory location. Other flags are altered according to the result of the operation.
Clock cycles = 15.

RLC (IX+d)

Rotates the contents of the memory location addressed by the contents of the IX register pair plus the offset d left by one bit position. The result is stored back at that position. The contents of bit 7 are copied into the carry flag and bit 0.

Code number   DD CB offset 06

The H and N flags are set to 0. The carry flag is set by bit 7 of the memory location. Other flags are set according to the result of the operation.
Clock cycles = 23.

RLC (IY+d)

Rotates the contents of the memory location addressed by the contents of the IY register pair plus the offset d left by one bit position. The result is stored back at that position. The contents of bit 7 are copied into the carry flag and bit 0.

Code number   FD CB offset 06

The H and N flags are set to 0. The carry flag is set by bit 7 of the memory location. Other flags are set according to the result of the operation.
Clock cycles = 23.

RLD

Performs a rotate left in BCD mode. Simultaneously, the 4 low bits of the memory location addressed by HL are moved to the 4 high bits of that location. The 4 high bits are moved to the 4 low bits of the accumulator. The 4 low bits of the accumulator are moved to the 4 low bits of the memory location.

Code number   ED 6F

The H and N flags are set to zero. The carry flag is not affected. Other flags are altered depending on the result of the operation.
Clock cycles = 18.

RR s

Rotates the contents of the operand s one bit position to the right. The carry flag is used as a 'ninth bit'. The contents of bit 0 are copied into the carry flag, and the contents of the carry flag are copied into bit 7.
There are several versions of this instruction.

Implicit A	CB 1F
Implicit B	CB 18
Implicit C	CB 19
Implicit D	CB 1A
Implicit E	CB 1B
Implicit H	CB 1C
Implicit L	CB 1D
Indirect (HL)	CB 1E
Indexed (IX+d)	DD CB offset 1E
Indexed (IY+d)	FD CB offset 1E

The H and N flags are set to zero. The carry flag is set by bit 0 of source. Other flags are altered depending on the result of the operation.
Clock cycles; implicit = 8, indirect = 15, indexed = 23.

RRA

The contents of the accumulator are rotated one bit position to the right. The carry flag is used as a 'ninth bit'. This instruction is the same as RR A, except for the effect on the flags.

Code number   1F

Flags H and N are set to 0. The carry flag is set by bit 0 of the accumulator. Other flags are unaffected.
Clock cycles = 4.

NB. This instruction is provided for compatibility with the 8080 processor.

RRC s

Rotates the contents of the specified operand one bit position to the right. The contents of bit 0 are copied into the carry flag and into bit 7.
There are several versions of this instruction.

Implicit A	CB 0F
Implicit B	CB 08
Implicit C	CB 09
Implicit D	CB 0A
Implicit E	CB 0B
Implicit H	CB 0C
Implicit L	CB 0D
Indirect (HL)	CB 0E
Indexed (IX+d)	DD CB offset 0E
Indexed (IY+d)	FD CB offset 0E

Flags H and N are set to zero. The carry flag is set by bit 0 of source. Other flags are altered depending on the result

of the operation.
Clock cycles; implicit = 8, indirect = 15, indexed = 23.

RRCA

Rotates the contents of the accumulator one bit position to the right. The contents of bit 0 are copied into the carry flag and into bit 7.

Code number   0F

The H and N flags are set to zero. The carry flag is set by bit 0 of the accumulator. Other flags are unaffected.
Clock cycles = 4.

RRD

Performs a rotate right in BCD mode. Simultaneously, the 4 high bits of the memory location addressed by the HL register pair are moved into the 4 low bits of that location. The 4 low bits are moved into the 4 low bits of the accumulator. The 4 low bits of the accumulator are moved into the 4 high bits of the memory location.

Code number   ED 67

The H and N flags are set to zero. The carry flag is unaffected. Other flags are set according to the results of the operation.
Clock cycles = 18.

RST p

Stores the contents of the program counter on the stack, and then loads the program counter with p. The next instruction is fetched from this address. This instruction can jump to one of eight addresses in low memory. It is used as a fast response to an interrupt.

p(Hex)	Code
00	C7
08	CF
10	D7
18	DF
20	E7
28	EF
30	F7
38	FF

No flags are affected.
Clock cycles = 11.

SBC A,s

Subtracts the contents of the specified operand s, plus the contents of the carry flag, from the accumulator. The result is stored in the accumulator.

There are several versions of this introduction.

Implicit A	9F
Implicit B	98
Implicit C	99
Implicit D	9A
Implicit E	9B
Implicit H	9C
Implicit L	9D
Immediate	DE data
Indirect (HL)	9E
Indexed (IX+d)	DD 9E offset
Indexed (IY+d)	FD 9E offset

The N flag is set to 1. Other flags may be altered depending on the result of the operation.

Clock cycles; implicit = 4, immediate = 7, indirect = 7, indexed = 19.

SBC HL,ss

Subtracts the contents of the specified register pair ss plus the carry flag from the contents of the register pair HL. The result is stored in HL.

Register code number	
BC	42
DE	52
HL	62
SP	72

The N flag is set to 1. The H flag is set if there is a borrow from bit 12. C is set if there is a borrow. Other flags are set according to the results of the operation.

Clock cycles = 15.

SCF

Sets the carry flag to 1.

Code number	37

The H and N flags are set to 0. The carry flag is set. Other flags are unaffected.

Clock cycles = 4.

SET b,r

This instruction sets to 1 the specified bit of the specified register.

The first byte is CB; the second byte is indicated in the following table:—

Register	A	B	C	D	E	H	L
Bit 0	C7	C0	C1	C2	C3	C4	C5
Bit 1	CF	C8	C9	CA	CB	CC	CD
Bit 2	D7	D0	D1	D2	D3	D4	D5
Bit 3	DF	D8	D9	DA	DB	DC	DD
Bit 4	E7	E0	E1	E2	E3	E4	E5
Bit 5	EF	E8	E9	EA	EB	EC	ED
Bit 6	F7	F0	F1	F2	F3	F4	F5
Bit 7	FF	F8	F9	FA	FB	FC	FD

The flags are not affected.
    Clock cycles = 8.

SET b,s

The specified bit of the specified memory location is set to 1.

Indirect (HL)	CB xx
Indexed (IX)	DD CB offset xx
Indexed (IY)	FD CB offset xx

Btye "xx" can be determined from the following list:—

Bit 0	C6
Bit 1	CE
Bit 2	D6
Bit 3	DE
Bit 4	E6
Bit 5	EE
Bit 6	F6
Bit 7	FE

The flags are not affected.

Clock cycles; indirect = 15, indexed = 23.

SLA s

The contents of the specified operand s are arithmetically shifted left by one bit position. Bit 7 is shifted into the carry flag, and bit 0 is forced to 0.

There are several versions of this instruction.

Implicit A	CB 27
Implicit B	CB 20
Implicit C	CB 21
Implicit D	CB 22
Implicit E	CB 23
Implicit H	CB 24
Implicit L	CB 25
Indirect (HL)	CB 26
Indexed (IX+d)	DD CB offset 26
Indexed (IY+d)	FD CB offset 26

The H and N flags are set to 0. The carry flag is set by bit 7 of source. Other flags may be altered depending on the result of the operation.

Clock cycles; implicit = 8, indirect = 15, indexed = 23.

SRA s

The contents of the specified operand s are arithmetically shifted right by one bit position. The contents of bit 0 are shifted into the carry flag. The contents of bit 7 are unchanged.

There are several versions of this instruction.

Implicit A	CB 2F
Implicit B	CB 28
Implicit C	CB 29
Implicit D	CB 2A
Implicit E	CB 2B
Implicit H	CB 2C
Implicit L	CB 2D
Indirect (HL)	CB 2E
Indexed (IX+d)	DD CB offset 2E
Indexed (IY+d)	FD CB offset 2E

The H and N flags are set to zero. The carry flag is set by bit 0 of source. Other flags may be altered depending on the result of the operation.

Clock cycles; implicit = 8, indirect = 15, indexed = 23.

SRL s

The contents of the specified operand s are logically shifted right by one bit position. The contents of bit 0 are moved into the carry flag and bit 7 is set to 0.

There are several versions of this instruction.

Implicit A	CB 3F
Implicit B	CB 38
Implicit C	CB 39
Implicit D	CB 3A
Implicit E	CB 3B
Implicit H	CB 3C
Implicit L	CB 3D
Indirect (HL)	CB 3E
Indexed (IX+d)	DD CB offset 3E
Indexed (IY+d)	FD CB offset 3E

The H and N flags are set to zero. The carry flag is set by bit 0 of source. Other flags may be altered by the result of the operation.

Clock cycles; implicit = 8, indirect = 15, indexed = 23.

SUB s

Subtracts the specified operand s from the accumulator, storing the result in the accumulator.

There are several versions of this instruction.

Implicit A	97
Implicit B	90
Implicit C	91
Implicit D	92
Implicit E	93
Implicit H	94
Implicit L	95
Immediate	D6 data
Indirect (HL)	96
Indexed (IX+d)	DD 96 offset
Indexed (IY+d)	FD 96 offset

The N flag is set to 1. Other flags may be altered depending on the result of the operation.

Clock cycles; implicit = 4, immediate = 7, indirect = 7, indexed = 19.

XOR s

Exclusive ORs the specified operand with the accumulator. The result is stored in the accumulator. XOR is performed according to the following rules on a bit-by-bit basis:—

1 XOR 1=0
1 XOR 0=1
0 XOR 0=0

There are several versions of this instruction.

Implicit A	AF
Implicit B	A8
Implicit C	A9
Implicit D	AA
Implicit E	AB
Implicit H	AC
Implicit L	AD
Immediate	EE data
Indirect (HL)	AE
Indexed (IX+d)	DD AE offset
Indexed (IY+d)	FD AE offset

The H, N, and C flags are set to zero. S, Z, and P may be altered depending on the result of the operation.

Clock cycles; implicit = 4, immediate = 7, indirect = 7, indexed = 19.

Chapter 4

STORING AND EXECUTION

The home computers with which this book is primarily concerned all have BASIC in ROM as their main language. BASIC normally expects to be able to use all the user-area of memory either for program storage or for variables.

In order to use machine code in these computers it is necessary to either find some way of protecting the code from being overwritten by BASIC, or to store the code in odd corners of the memory map which are normally not used either by BASIC or by the operating system.

The Memotech MTX computers are the most helpful in this respect. Not only do they have built-in assemblers, but they also automatically take care of storing the assembled machine code. It is, in fact, stored within the BASIC program area of memory.

With the Sinclair ZX computers and the Amstrad CPC 464, no such in-built method exists. With these computers, different approaches are necessary depending on whether only a short routine or a longer machine code program is to be stored.

With short routines, a very simple method of storage is to use a REM at the very beginning of the program. This can initially be filled with any character. The machine code is then POKEd into the area of memory occuped by these characters either from DATA statements when the program is run, or directly from command mode a byte at a time. This byte-at-a-time method is time-consuming, but worthwhile on a computer like the ZX-81, which has a very small memory in its basic form, and which in any case does not have READ and DATA statements in its' BASIC.

The advantage of the REM method is that, when the program is recorded on disc or tape, the machine code in the REM is recorded with it.

The REM must be at the start of the program, both to make it easy to locate, and to prevent it moving if the BASIC program is edited.

Odd corners of memory tend not to be very satisfactory. For a start, they tend to be very small, perhaps 10 or 20 bytes. Secondly, computer manufacturers tend to modify their products from time to time, sometimes unannounced, and an unused corner can suddenly find employment. This means that a program using this storage method may not work on all versions of a machine.

The best method of storing substantial machine code programs is to store them above the area used by BASIC. To do this, the area used by BASIC must be reduced, by lowering the highest memory location available to BASIC. The address of this location is stored in RAM, and can be POKEd to a lower value. There may be a BASIC statement to do this, such as CLEAR on the Spectrum and MEMORY on the Amstrad CPC 464. The space thus created will hold machine code safe from corruption, in most cases even if a new program is loaded. The address of the memory location(s) to be altered will normally be found in the manual for your computer, usually in an appendix (System Variables).

Execution

Putting the machine code in memory is the first step. The second is to cause it to be executed. Whether in a program or from command mode, this normally has to be done with a BASIC statement.

The simplest statement to use is CALL. This command is followed by the start address of the machine code routine. The routine must be terminated by an RET instruction (not matched to a JSR within the routine) to cause a return to BASIC. Unfortunately, very few Z80 BASICs support this statement, the LOCOMOTIVE BASIC in the Amstrad being an exception.

The alternative statement is USR. This executes a machine-code routine which is supposed to return a numeric value to the program, which is deposited in a variable or printed. This statement takes the general form A=USR(AAAA), where AAAA is the start address. The USR statement varies considerably from computer to computer and reference to your computer's manual for details is advised. In many Z80-based computers, including the Sinclair ZX models and the Memotechs, the value returned by USR is the contents of the BC register pair, regarded as an unsigned integer. The Amstrad CPC 464 does not have the USR statement. Generally, return to BASIC is again by an RET instruction.

Chapter 5

EXAMPLE PROGRAMS

The short demonstration programs in this chapter will be given in standard Z-80 assembly language form.

BASIC listings to enable the programs to be entered and run on 4 popular Z-80 based home computers are also given. In the case of the Memotech, these use the in-built assembler. The Sinclair Spectrum and Amstrad programs use DATA statements, and a loader program is given for the ZX81.

If you have an assembler for your computer, you should be able to enter the programs for the assembly language listings.

1. ADD

This program adds together two 8-bit numbers, i.e. they must be more than 255. The result, of course, can be up to 510, so the answer may need two bytes. In fact, the answer is placed in the BC register pair, so this routine can be executed with the USR statement (in fact this is true of all these demonstration programs except the Amstrad versions, which have an extra instruction to place the contents of the BC pair in memory locations at the end of the program, where they can be retrieved by PEEKs).

```
LD B,0
LD A,(N1LOC)
LD D,A
LD A,(N2LOC)
```

```
              ADD D
              LD C,A
              JR NC OUT
              INC B
OUT           RET
```

The two numbers to be added are POKEd into two memory locations which I have called N1LOC and N2LOC. In actually entering the program, you would substitute the actual addresses. The first number is loaded first into the accumulator, and then into the D register. The second number is then loaded into the accumulator, and the contents of D added. The result is then stored in the C register. If a carry resulted, the B register, (set to 0 at the start of the routine) is incremented. Otherwise, the routine branches directly to OUT, which is where it terminates. A jump relative is used rather than a jump absolute, as this makes the program relocatable in memory. The result returned is 256*the content of the B register, + the contents of the C register.

2. AND

This program performs the Boolean AND operation on two 8-bit numbers. In essence, it is very similar to the addition program, except the result is always an 8-bit number, so there is no need for a conditional jump.

This program can also be easily modified to perform OR and XOR by changing the appropriate instruction (and one word in the BASIC program).

```
              LD B,0
              LD A,(N1LOC)
              LD D,A
              LD A,(N2LOC)
```

```
        AND D
        LD C,A
        RET
```

This routine may prove useful, as the Sinclair and Memotech AND and OR functions do not work on a bitwise basis.

3. LOOP

This program illustrates a loop structure in machine code, and is functionally equivalent to the following BASIC program:—

```
10 LET T=0
20 FOR C=1 TO 255
30 LET T=T+C
40 NEXT C
50 PRINT T
```

It is instructive to run both the BASIC and machine-code versions and compare the time taken. The BASIC version takes several seconds (longer on the ZX81), whereas the machine code is virtually instantaneous.

```
        LD B,0
        LD C,0
        LD D,0
LOOP    INC D
        LD A,D
        ADD A,C
        LD C,A
        JR NC,OVER
        INC B
```

```
OVER        LD A,255
            CP D
            JR NZ,LOOP
            RET
```

The BC register pair is equivalent to the BASIC variable T (total), and the D register is equivalent to the BASIC variable C (counter). At the start of each loop, the D register is incremented (which is why it is initialised to 0 rather than 1). It is then loaded into the accumulator, and added to the contents of the C register. The result is then loaded into the C register. (A common mistake among beginners to machine code/assembly language is forgetting to store the results of operations — you have been warned!). If a carry resulted from the addition, the B register is incremented. The D register is then compared with the limit, 255, which is loaded into the accumulator. When D is equal to 255, the comparison will set the zero flag. The loop continues until that happens.

4. TAKE

This program performs a subtraction between two 16-bit numbers. It uses unsigned arithmetic, so the second number must be smaller than the first. That is, the result must not be negative.

```
            LD HL,(N1LOC)
            LD DE,(N2LOC)
            SBC HL,DE
            LD B,H
            LD C,L
            RET
```

The first two instructions load the register pairs directly with the 16-bit numbers. The addresses N1LOC and N2LOC are therefore the addresses of the first pairs of bytes. The third instruction performs the 16-bit subtraction, leaving the result in the HL pair. Two instructions are necessary to transfer this result into the BC register pair.

When using pairs of bytes to hold 16-bit numbers, the most important thing is to make sure you always get the high-order and low-order bytes the right way round.

MACHINE SPECIFIC LISTINGS
Memotech Versions
ADD

```
10 CODE

8007              NOP
8008              NOP
8009              LD B,0
800B              LD A,(32775)
800E              LD D,A
800F              LD A,(32776)
8012              ADD A,D
8013              LD C,A
8014              JR NC,OUT
8016              INC B
8017 OUT:         RET
8018              RET

Symbols:
OUT8017
```

20 INPUT "First Number? ";N1
30 POKE 32775,N1

```
40 INPUT "Second Number? ";N2
50 POKE 32776,N2
60 PRINT
70 PRINT N1;" + ";N2;" = ";USR(32777)
80 PRINT : PRINT
90 GOTO 20
```

AND

```
10 CODE
```

8007	NOP
8008	NOP
8009	LD B,0
800B	LD A,(32775)
800E	LD D,A
800F	LD A,(32776)
8012	AND D
8013	LD C,A
8014	RET

Symbols:

```
20 INPUT "First Number? ";N1
30 POKE 32775,N1
40 INPUT "Second Number? ";N2
50 POKE 32776,N2
60 PRINT
70 PRINT N1;" AND ";N2;" = ";USR(32777)
80 PRINT:PRINT
90 GOTO 20
```

LOOP

10 CODE

```
8007           LD B,0
8009           LD C,0
800B           LD D,0
800D LOOP:     INC D
800E           LD A,D
800F           ADD A,C
8010           LD C,A
8011           JR NC,OVER
8013           INC B
8014 OVER:     LD A,255
8016           CP D
8017           JR NZ,LOOP
8019           RET
```

Symbols:
LOOP800DOVER8014

20 PRINT USR(32775)

TAKE

10 CODE

```
8007           LD HL,(32787)
800A           LD DE,(32789)
800E           SBC HL,DE
8010           LD B,H
```

8011	LD C,L
8012	RET
8013	INC D
8014	NOP
8015	LD A,(BC)
8016	NOP
8017	RET

Symbols:


```
20 INPUT "FIRST NUMBER? ";N1
30 POKE 32787,MOD(N1,256)
40 POKE 32788,INT(N1/256)
50 INPUT "SECOND NUMBER? ";N2
60 POKE 32789,MOD(N2,256)
70 POKE 32790,INT(N2/256)
80 PRINT
90 PRINT N1;"−";N2;" = ";USR(32775)
100 PRINT : PRINT
110 GOTO 20
```

ZX81 Versions

ZX81 Loader Program

```
1 REM (ENOUGH CHARACTERS TO
    TAKE THE MACHINE CODE)
10 LET M=16514
20 INPUT V
30 POKE M,V
```

```
40 PRINT PEEK(M)
50 LET M=M+1
60 GOTO 20
```

Use this program to enter all the machine code numbers, then enter STOP. You can then replace lines 10 to 60 with the BASIC programs. Be sure to put sufficient characters in the REM in line 1.

ADD

MACHINE CODE:—
0,0,6,0,58,130,64,87,58,131,64,130,79,48,1,4,201

BASIC:—
```
10 PRINT "FIRST NUMBER?"
20 INPUT N1
30 POKE 16514,N1
40 PRINT "SECOND NUMBER?"
50 INPUT N2
60 POKE 16515,N2
70 PRINT N1;" + ";N2;" = ";USR 16516
80 GOTO 20
```

AND

MACHINE CODE:—
0,0,6,0,58,130,64,87,58,131,64,162,79,201

BASIC:—
```
10 PRINT "FIRST NUMBER?"
20 INPUT N1
```

```
30 POKE 16514,N1
40 PRINT "SECOND NUMBER?"
50 INPUT N2
60 POKE 16515,N2
70 PRINT N1;" AND ";N2;" = ";USR 16516
80 GOTO 20
```

LOOP

MACHINE CODE:—
6,0,14,0,22,0,20,122,129,79,48,1,4,62,255,186,32,244,201

Having entered this code, execute the program with
PRINT USR 16514 in direct mode.

TAKE

MACHINE CODE:—
0,0,0,0,42,130,64,237,91,132,64,237,82,68,77,201

BASIC:—
```
10 PRINT "FIRST NUMBER?"
20 INPUT N1
30 LET V1=INT(N1/256)
40 LET V2=N1−256*V1
50 POKE 16514,V2
60 POKE 16515,V1
70 PRINT "SECOND NUMBER?"
80 INPUT N2
90 LET V1=INT(N2/256)
```

```
100 LET V2=N2−256*V1
110 POKE 16516,V2
120 POKE 16517,V1
130 PRINT
140 PRINT N1;"−";N2;" = ";USR 16518
150 PRINT
160 GOTO 10
```

N.B. The zeros at the start of the machine code numbers are the bytes that are used to pass the numbers to the machine code routines. You are recommended to always reset these to zero before trying to list the programs.

ZX Spectrum Versions

Enter CLEAR 32499 and NEW before typing in the following programs.

ADD

```
10 FOR M=32502 TO 32520
20 READ V
30 POKE M,V
40 NEXT M
50 DATA 6,0,58,244,126,87,58,245,126,130,
        79,48,1,4,201
60 INPUT "First number? ";N1
70 POKE 32500,N1
80 INPUT "Second number? ";N2
90 POKE 32501,N2
100 PRINT N1;" + ";N2;" = ";USR 32502
110 PRINT
120 GOTO 60
```

AND

```
10 FOR M=32502 TO 32513
20 READ V
30 POKE M,V
40 NEXT M
50 DATA 6,0,58,244,126,87,58,245,126,162,79,201
60 INPUT "First number? ";N1
70 POKE 32500,N1
80 INPUT "Second number? ";N2
90 POKE 32501,N2
100 PRINT N1;" AND ";N2;" = ";USR 32502
110 PRINT
120 GOTO 60
```

LOOP

```
10 FOR M=32500 TO 32518
20 READ V
30 POKE M,V
40 NEXT M
50 DATA 6,0,14,0,22,0,20,122
60 DATA 129,79,48,1,4,62,255,186
70 DATA 32,244,201
80 PRINT "Press a key"
90 IF INKEY$="" THEN GOTO 90
100 PRINT USR 32500
```

TAKE

```
10 FOR M=32504 TO 32515
```

```
20 READ V
30 POKE M,V
40 NEXT M
50 DATA 42,244,126,237,91,246,126,237,
      82,68,77,201
60 INPUT "First number? ";N1
70 LET V1=INT (N1/256)
80 LET V2=N1-256*V1
90 POKE 32500,V2
100 POKE 32501,V1
110 INPUT "Second number? ";N2
120 LET V1=INT (N2/256)
130 LET V2=N2-256*V1
140 POKE 32502,V2
150 POKE 32503,V1
160 PRINT
170 PRINT N1;"-";N2;" = ";USR 32504
180 PRINT
190 GOTO 60
```

Amstrad CPC 464 Versions

ADD

```
10 MEMORY 32499
20 FOR m=32502 TO 32520
30 READ v
40 POKE m,v
50 NEXT m
60 DATA 6,0,58,244,126,87,58,245,126,130,
      79,48,1,4,237,67,9,127,201
```

117

```
70 INPUT "First Number";nl
80 POKE 32500,nl
90 INPUT "Second Number";n2
100 POKE 32501,n2
110 CALL 32502
120 PRINT n1;" + ";n2;" = ";PEEK(32521)
        +256*PEEK(32522)
130 PRINT
140 GOTO 60
```

AND

```
10 MEMORY 32499
20 FOR m=32502 TO 32517
30 READ v
40 POKE m,v
50 NEXT m
60 DATA 6,0,58,244,126,87,58,245,126,162,79,
        237,67,6,127,201
70 INPUT "First Number";nl
80 POKE 32500,nl
90 INPUT "Second Number";n2
100 POKE 32501,n2
110 CALL 32502
120 PRINT n1;" AND ";n2;" = ";PEEK(32518)
130 PRINT
140 GOTO 70
```

LOOP

```
10 MEMORY 32499
20 FOR m=32500 TO 32522
```

```
30 READ v
40 POKE m,v
50 NEXT m
60 DATA 6,0,14,0,22,0,20,122,129,79
70 DATA 48,1,4,62,255,186,32,244
80 DATA 236,67,11,127,201
90 PRINT "PRESS ANY KEY"
100 CALL 32500
120 PRINT PEEK(32523)+256*PEEK(32524)
```

TAKE

```
10 MEMORY 32499
20 FOR m=32504 TO 32519
30 READ v
40 POKE m,v
50 NEXT m
60 DATA 42,244,126,237,91,246,126,237,
       82,68,77,237,67,8,127,201
70 INPUT "First Number";nl
80 LET vl=INT(nl/256)
90 LET v2=n1−256*v1
100 POKE 32500,v2
110 POKE 32501,v1
120 INPUT "Second Number";n2
130 LET v1=INT(n2/256)
140 LET v2=n2−256*v1
150 POKE 32502,v2
160 POKE 32503,v1
170 PRINT
```

```
180 CALL 32504
190 PRINT nl;"– ";n2;" = ";PEEK(32520)
       +256*PEEK(32521)
200 GOTO 70
```

Chapter 6
INPUT/OUTPUT

When using a high level language such as BASIC, commands to control input/output devices such as the CRT controller and printer port are normally provided, or they may be included in the form of operating system commands. In either case the user is not directly accessing registers of the input/output devices, and is unlikely to need any knowledge of the way in which they function. The situation is totally different with machine code, and in order to take advantage of the speed of machine code programs it is often necessary to directly access and control peripheral devices. This can be a little difficult at first, even for someone who is used to dealing with electronic circuits, since the methods adopted in most computer peripherals are rather different to those used in non-computer electronic circuits. However, once a few fundamental points have been grasped it is not too difficult to use and understand practically any computer peripheral device.

Even just restricting ourselves to peripherals for use with the Z80 and Z80A microprocessors, there are many devices in common use and it would not be feasable to even briefly describe all of these complex devices here. Fortunately, the basic way in which these devices are controlled varies little from one type to another, and by taking just a brief look at just one computer peripheral a number of important and universal points can be unveiled.

The Z80CTC

As an example of a peripheral integrated circuit for use with the Z80 we will consider the Z80CTC (the Z80ACTC is the high speed version for use with Z80A based systems). CTC simply stands for counter timer circuit, and it can be used in a number of counting and timer applications in a computer system. We will not consider the device in great detail here, since it has a great many features which would take many pages to fully explain. However, the device consists basically of four 8 bit counter timer circuits with a prescaler for each one. It has the pinout configuration shown in Figure 4. D0 to D7 connect to the data bus of the system, and data is sent to and received from the chip via these terminals. Some of the other lines (IORQ and MI for examples) are control lines which are fed from the corresponding lines of the microprocessor. CS0 and CS1 are the two channel select inputs, which are used to select the desired channel by feeding them with the appropriate 2 bit binary address (there are four channels which are numbered from 0 to 3). CS0 and CS1 are normally fed from address lines A0 to A1 respectively. CE is the chip enable input, and this is operated from address lines A2 to A7 and some of the control bus lines via a suitable decoder circuit. This places the CTC at four consecutive addresses in the in/out map. For instance, the internal Z80ACTC circuit of the Memotech MTX500 and MTX512 computers is at in/out addresses 8 to 11, and data can be either written to or read from each of these addresses. Remember that the Z80/Z80A uses separate memory and input/output maps, and that the instructions used with peripheral devices are different to the instructions used when accessing memory.

There are two main ways of using each counter/timer circuit of the Z80CTC/Z80ACTC. One is to count input pulses on the relevant clock/trigger input. The second mode is the more common one, and it is where the system clock signal is divided by the circuit to give an output at a

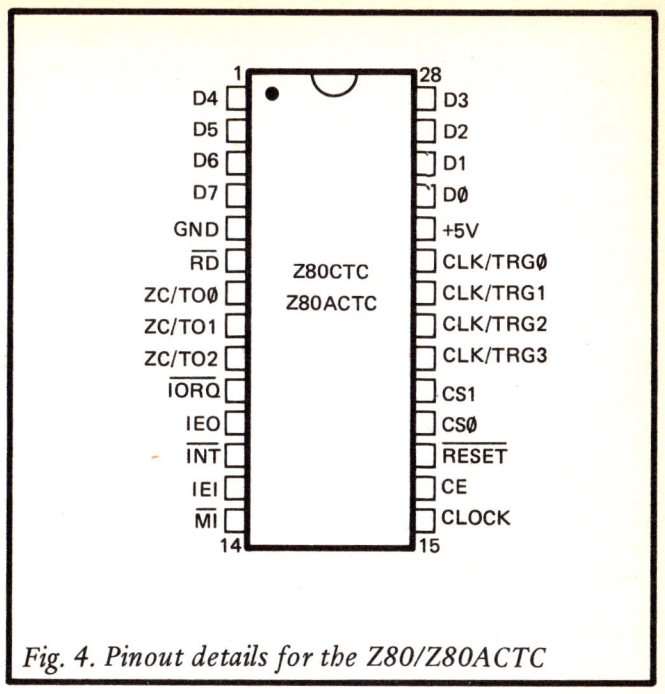

Fig. 4. Pinout details for the Z80/Z80ACTC

lower frequency. This feature can be used to give a range of clock frequencies (and baud rates) for a serial interface, or to provide the computer with a timer function. For example, if the CTC circuit is used to provide a divide by 40000 action with a 4MHz clock signal, this would give timing signals at intervals of one hundredth of a second. This could be used to increment a memory location (or series of locations) one hundred times a second with the aid of interrupts and a suitable interrupt routine.

Control Register

So how is the required operating mode selected? There are no pins which can be used to program the device, and it is in fact done under software control by writing data to the control registers of the device. Let us assume that we wish to use timer 2 in the mode where it divides the clock signal, and that we wish to divide by 2560. There are two divider stages in each channel, one of which is a simple prescaler which divides the signal by 1, 16, or 256. The other is an 8 bit counter which divides by any integer from 1 to 256. The division rate provided by this register is equal to the number written to it, except where 0 is sent (this gives a division rate of 256).

There is a slight complication here in that each timer/counter occupies just one address, and the control register and the 8 bit divider register therefore share the same address. This problem is overcome by first writing to the control register of the appropriate channel, and then writing to the counter. First the data to the control register is sent, with bit 0 being set high to indicate that the data is to be stored in the control register, and bit 2 being set high to indicate that the next byte written to that address is to be loaded into the counter circuit. Other bits of the control register control other functions, and bit 1 is set to 0 to allow operation of the counter, or high to inhibit it. In this case bit 1 must obviously be set low. Some of the control register bits are not very relevant in this mode of operation, but bit 6 is of importance. This is set high to set the prescaler in the divide by 1 mode (effectively eliminating it), or low to set the prescaler in the divide by 16 or 256 mode. Assuming bit 6 is set low, bit 5 then determines whether the prescaler is in the divide by 16 (set to 0) or the divide by 256 (set to 1) mode.

In this case we require the prescaler in the divide by 256 mode, with 10 written to the counter circuit, giving the required total division rate of 2560. We must therefore set bits 0, 2, and 5 high in order to set the desired mode of operation, which gives a total 37 (1 + 4 + 32 = 37) to write to the control register. Then the value of 10 would be written to the counter as the same address. In order to set a new division rate data would again be written to the control register to set the mode of operation (even if it had not changed) and then the number to the counter would be sent.

This method of having more than one register at each address is not something that is common to every peripheral device, but it is not a rarity either. In the read mode there is in fact only one register at each address, and a read operation always returns data from the counter and not from the control register. The two important concepts here are the use of bits of a control register to set a peripheral device in the desired operating mode, and writing data to or reading it from a peripheral device in much the same way as data is written to and taken from memory (but using the special input/output instructions of course).

The (positive) output pulses are obtained on the zero counter/timeout pin of the relevant channel, but as mentioned earlier, and alternative to using this signal is to use the device to generate an interrupt. This is done by setting the interrupt enable bit to 1, and this is bit 7 of each control register. As mentioned in an earlier chapter, in two interrupt modes the device generating the interrupt has to provide the low byte of the first of two addresses where the start address of the interrupt routine is stored. In actual fact the least significant bit is always 0, but the interrupting device must supply the other seven bits. With the Z80CTC/Z80ACTC the interrupt vector is loaded by writing the appropriate value to channel 0 (with the least significant bit set at 0). In this case the CTC sets bits 1 and 2 automatically so that priority is given to channel 0, through to minimum priority for channel 3. This enables each channel to have its own interrupt routine, giving maximum versatility.

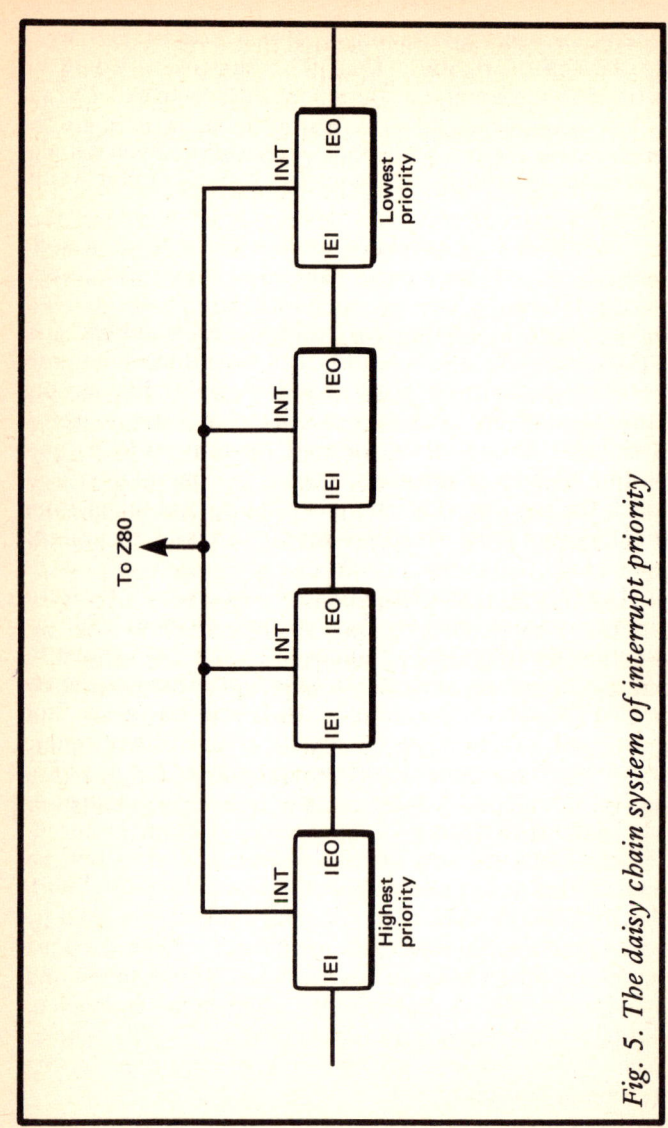

Fig. 5. The daisy chain system of interrupt priority

You will often come across the term daisy chain interrupts when dealing with Z80/Z80A peripheral devices. This is where several devices which generate interrupts are connected together in the manner shown in Figure 5. The idea is simply that the device which is closest to the microprocessor has the highest priority, since it blocks signals from other devices from reaching the microprocessor until its own interrupt routine has been serviced. This gives a chain of priority, with the highest priority being given to the devices close to the microprocessor, and the lowest of those that are furthest away.

When using a high level language such as BASIC the programmer is largely isolated from the hardware of the computer by some sophisticated software. When using machine code this software is absent, and the programmer has to deal directly with the devices in the machine unless it is acceptable to revert to BASIC when dealing with these devices (which will not always be the case). With many machine code applications it is therefore necessary to have a good understanding of the computer you are using, and its hardware, and you should try to find as much information of this type as possible. You may well find it useful to obtain data sheets on some of the peripheral devices in the machine. If you are in doubt about the correct way of programming and using a peripheral device, in most cases a little experimentation will soon clarify matters.

Notes

OTHER BOOKS OF INTEREST

BP112: A Z80 WORKSHOP MANUAL
E.A. Parr, B.Sc., C.Eng., M.I.E.E.

Intended for people who wish to progress beyond the stage of BASIC programming to topics such as machine code and assembly language programming or need hardware details of the Z80 based computer.

Starting with a review of computer principles, the book describes typical machine code instructions followed by a detailed description of the Z80 instruction set. Assembly language programming is discussed with examples.

Also given are hardware details of the Z80 and the use of associated. I/O devices such as UARTs. PIOs and CTCs.

This book is not purely a descriptive text, however, Z80 hex machine code and assembler instructions are given in tabular form, along with in/out connections for Z80 and associated devices. It will therefore also be a useful reference book for the more experienced user.

192 pages   *1983*
ISBN 0 85934 087 2   **£2.75**

BP119: THE ART OF PROGRAMMING THE ZX SPECTRUM
M. James, B.Sc., M.B.C.S.

The incredible ZX Spectrum presents its user with virtually unlimited scope. It allows versatile use of colour, offers high and low resolution graphics and also adds sound. The result can mean some very effective and exciting programs from BASIC — if you just know how!

The problem is that there is a little more than meets the eye in getting your Spectrum to do clever things. It is one thing to have learnt how to use all the Spectrum's commands but a very different one to be able to combine them into progrms that do exactly what you want them to. This is just what this book is all about — teaching you the art of effective programming with your Spectrum.

The Text is divided into the following chapters: 1, Getting to Know Your Spectrum; 2, Low Resolution Graphics; 3, Fun at Random; 4, High Resolution Graphics; 5, Sound; 6, Moving Graphics; 7, PEEK and POKE; 8, A Sense of Time; 9, Strings and Words; 10, Advanced Graphics.

Essential Reading for all Spectrum users be they beginners or seasoned programmers.

144 pages   *1983*
ISBN 0 85934 094 5   **£2.50**

BP153: AN INTRODUCTION TO PROGRAMMING THE AMSTRAD CPC464

R.A. & J.W. Penfold

The excellent hardware of the Amstrad CPC 464 running with Locomotive BASIC go to make up an extremely potent and versatile machine and this book has been written to help the reader expand the potential of this powerful combination, with the minimum of difficulty.

The authors adopt a step-by-step approach starting with the fundamentals and then moving on to more advanced topics, with many example programs being included to illustrate and clarify points.

In a book of this size it is impossible to fully cover every aspect of a machine as complex as the Amstrad CPC464, but the authors have tried, as far as possible, to complement the information supplied by the manufacturer rather than just duplicate it.

The text is divided into the following chapters: 1, Variables & Arrays; 2, String Variables; 3, Decisions; 4, INPUT, PRINT & DATA; 5, The Sound Generator; 6, Graphics 1 — Modes & Colours; 7, Graphics 2 — Animation; 8, Binary & Hex; 9, Interfacing; 10, Interrupts.

144 pages   *1984*
ISBN 0 85934 128 3   **£2.25**

Please note adjacent and overleaf is a list of other titles that are available in our range of Radio, Electronics and Computer Books.

These should be available from all good Booksellers, Radio Component Dealers and Mail Order Companies.

However, should you experience difficulty in obtaining any title in your area, then please write directly to the publisher enclosing payment to cover the cost of the book plus adequate postage.

If you would like a complete catalogue of our entire range of Radio, Electronics and Computer Books then please send a Stamped Addressed Envelope to:

BERNARD BABANI (publishing) LTD
THE GRAMPIANS
SHEPHERDS BUSH ROAD
LONDON W6 7NF
ENGLAND